Ship
Ashore!

SIGNALLING AT NIGHT.

A United States lifesaver signals a vessel at night. Engraving from *Harper's Weekly* (1888).

Ship Ashore!

The U.S. Lifesavers of Coastal North Carolina

JOE A. MOBLEY

40494

Division of Archives and History
North Carolina Department of Cultural Resources
Raleigh
1994

For Kay

Contents

Foreword

The romance of the sea has generated many stories of heroism and courage over the years, but few can compete with the true-life exploits of the United States lifesavers. In a work of original research, Joe A. Mobley recounts the story of North Carolina's lifesavers and the service they performed along the state's treacherous coast. The rescue of shipwrecked mariners has contributed much to the lore and charm of the Outer Banks.

Mr. Mobley brings the experienced insight of a skilled historian to the story of the United States lifesavers of coastal North Carolina. For two decades he has worked at a variety of jobs in the Division of Archives and History as an archivist, historical researcher for the State Historic Preservation Office, records analyst, and editor. Among his publications are *James City: A Black Community in North Carolina, 1863-1900* (1981) and *Pamlico County: A Brief History* (1991). He currently is completing editorial work on volume 2 of *The Papers of Zebulon Baird Vance*. Mr. Mobley received both his bachelor's and master's degrees from North Carolina State University.

Jeffrey J. Crow
Historical Publications Administrator

February 1994

Acknowledgments

The author expresses his appreciation to several persons whose time and effort helped ensure the publication of this study. He is grateful to Jeffrey J. Crow and Wilson Angley for reading the draft and offering a number of helpful suggestions. Robert J. Cain brought to the author's attention new sources concerning early shipwrecks in North Carolina. Charles Edward Morris and Stephen E. Massengill assisted with records and photographs. Robert M. Topkins and Lisa D. Bailey went over the page proofs with close editorial scrutiny, and Mr. Topkins indexed the volume. Seaman Scott Palmer of the Oak Island Coast Guard Station provided an informative tour and discussion of that facility and its equipment. The author especially wishes to thank Kathleen B. (Kay) Wyche, who edited the manuscript, prepared maps, took photographs, and designed and typeset the book.

Patroling Barnegat

Wild, wild the storm, and the sea high running,
Steady the roar of the gale, with incessant undertone muttering,
Shouts of demoniac laughter fitfully piercing and pealing,
Waves, air, midnight, their savagest trinity lashing,
Out in the shadows there milk-white combs careering,
On beachy slush and sand spirts of snow fierce slanting,
Where through the murk the easterly death-wind breasting,
Through cutting swirl and spray watchful and firm advancing,
(That in the distance! is that a wreck? is the red signal flaring?)
Slush and sand of the beach tireless till daylight wending,
Steadily, slowly, through hoarse roar never remitting,
Along the midnight edge by those milk-white combs careering,
A group of dim, weird forms, struggling, the night confronting,
The savage trinity warily watching.

—Walt Whitman

A United States lifesaving station operated at Barnegat, N.J., where Whitman sometimes visited. This poem appeared first in the *American* in June 1880, in *Harper's Monthly* in April 1881, and then among the "Sea-Drift" series in Whitman's *Leaves of Grass* (7th ed., 1881).

Introduction

The coast of North Carolina is both beautiful and dangerous. Like some siren of classical literature, it has lured many an unsuspecting seafarer to his death with its seductive song of calm solitude. The Outer Banks, a chain of windswept sand islands, stretch along the coastline from the Virginia border to Cape Lookout. Over the years, as weather and currents fluctuated and the sea rose and fell, inlets opened and closed along these banks, which are separated from the mainland by a number of shallow sounds. Below Cape Lookout a series of sand reefs, islands, and inlets continues southward to the major port of Wilmington, the precarious Cape Fear and Frying Pan Shoals, and finally the South Carolina line. Visitors—from the earliest explorers of the sixteenth century to twentieth-century tourists—have been struck by coastal North Carolina's natural majesty. In 1524 Giovanni da Verrazano, a Florentine navigator in the service of France, explored the area from Cape Fear to present-day Kitty Hawk and, in the earliest description known of the Atlantic coast north of Cape Fear, reported that it was "as pleasant and delectable to behold, as is possible to imagine." Today vacationers, retirees, and even long-time residents are lured and impressed by the balmy weather, the sunbathed beaches that seem to stretch forever, and the green lushness and fascinating marine and animal life of the sounds and marshes. But beneath that facade of calm beauty lurk elements of death and destruction, which can erupt suddenly and in a way that occurs at no other place on the Atlantic coast.

Geographically, North Carolina occupies a spot unique in the Western Hemisphere. Located in the center of the Outer Banks, Cape Hatteras extends so far into the Atlantic Ocean that it reaches the northbound Gulf Stream, which skirts the Carolina coast just before turning out to sea. At that meeting site the warm waters of the stream and the cold waters of the southbound Labrador Current collide, creating vicious, stormlike turbulence and thereby forming the fearsome Diamond Shoals. The shifting sands of the shoals, combined with tremendously violent storms excited by the volatile mixture of warm and cold water, have for generations mercilessly destroyed large numbers of ships and killed their ill-fated crews. The conditions at Diamond Shoals, along with those at other sites nearly as perilous, such as Cape Lookout Shoals and Frying Pan Shoals, have claimed so many shipwrecks that the North Carolina coast has earned the name Graveyard of the Atlantic. Throughout the nautical history of the Atlantic Seaboard, many ships' captains and sailors departed aboard vessels from safe harbors north or south of North Carolina with only the prospect of fair weather and smooth sailing before them. Upon reaching the dreaded Graveyard of the Atlantic, however, they soon found their worst fears realized as they were suddenly caught in a nightmarish caldron of rain, wind, and storm that seemed to come from nowhere atop rolling, crushing waves. Year after year for over three centuries countless ships continued to descend into underwater graves in North Carolina's maritime burial ground. There they still rest, eerie reminders of nature's violence. Sometimes, even today, at low tide the skeletal corpses—or perhaps just a mast or funnel—of those once-living and -working ships can be seen from the beach. David Stick, the foremost historian of the Outer Banks and their shipwrecks, has concluded that 650

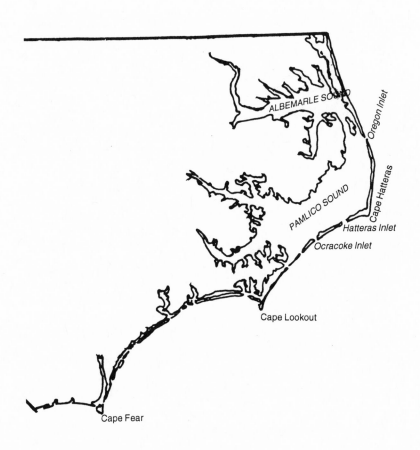

NORTH CAROLINA COASTLINE

verifiable vessels have been totally lost off the North Carolina coast. One can only guess how many more unverified and less-than-total losses may have occurred in four centuries of North Carolina history.

For a long time little could be done to prevent such disasters or to rescue their victims. Today, of course, these responsibilities fall to the United States Coast Guard. Every resident of coastal North Carolina knows—and every visitor soon learns—of the important role that the Coast Guard has played in the region. Having a long and illustrious tradition dating back to the nation's beginning, the modern Coast Guard (organized as an agency with that specific name in 1915) presently performs a dual mission. Existing for most of its career as part of the United States Department of the Treasury but serving under the Department of Transportation since 1967, the Coast Guard enforces the country's customs and immigration laws and ensures that all shipping and boating interests comply with United States maritime rules and regulations. The organization also serves as a rescue service for vessels and their crews that become imperiled by weather conditions or other dangerous and unforeseen circumstances. The Coast Guard has distinguished itself in both roles, as well as serving in conjunction with the United States Navy in time of war.

But before 1915 the federal agency that was the forerunner of the modern Coast Guard did not always have the authority or capability to perform lifesaving duties. In fact, when the United States government created its first "coast guard" in 1789, it did not include rescue operations as part of the new organization's mission. In that year Congress passed a law to establish within the Department of the Treasury a division to function as a type of "floating police service" to assist that department in regulating "the collection of duties imposed by law on the tonnage of ships or vessels, and on goods, wares and merchandises imported into the United States." The 1789 act made no mention of saving lives at sea.

The newly organized service, which originally did not have a statutory designation, was called the "Revenue Service," the "Revenue Marine," the "Revenue Marine Service," or the "System of Cutters," after Congress in 1790 appropriated funds for ten cutters for use in enforcing customs laws. As early as 1832 the secretary of the treasury referred to the organization as the "Revenue Cutter Service." Five years later the service began officially using its cutters for rescue and assistance to vessels in distress, as well as for enforcing customs and maritime laws, suppressing the foreign slave trade, and ensuring quarantines. Then in 1863 Congress gave the agency the statutory name "United States Revenue Cutter Service," although that title continued to be used interchangeably with the usually preferred term "Revenue Marine Service" until 1894, when "Revenue Cutter Service" became the almost universally accepted designation. That one was in use in 1915, when the present-day Coast Guard was formed.

But regardless of what it was called, the oldest ancestor of the modern Coast Guard remained for most of its career an agency primarily concerned with law enforcement, with little time or means to perform coastal rescue. Not until the 1870s did the federal government officially establish a component of the Department of the Treasury exclusively committed to the systematic saving of shipwrecked victims—the United States Lifesaving Service.

The Lifesaving Service began operating on the coast of North Carolina in 1874, and ultimately twenty-nine lifesaving stations, manned by North Carolinians (white and black), stood along the treacherous Tar Heel coastline from Wash Woods in the north to Oak Island in the south. The following chapters are devoted to a discussion of the events leading to the establishment of those outposts and to the role of their gallant lifesavers in the maritime history of North Carolina.

Chapter 1
The Savage Trinity

Shipwrecks and the desperate need for means of rescuing the victims of such disasters have been a part of the history of North Carolina since the sixteenth century. When a Spanish expedition led by explorer Lucas Vázquez de Ayllón unsuccessfully attempted to plant a colony on the Cape Fear River in 1526, one of its ships wrecked at the treacherous mouth of the river, forcing the expedition to build a replacement. In 1585 the flagship *Tiger*—a part of the fleet transporting Sir Walter Raleigh's colonists to Roanoke Island, site of the first English colony in the New World—stranded and then was repaired and refloated at Ocracoke Island. Other vessels sank at Cape Fear in 1665 and at Cape Lookout in the following year. But in all probability no one will ever be able to estimate even closely the number of ships that may have grounded or sunk off North Carolina in the seventeenth century. During that era Spanish frigates and galleons laden with gold, silver, sugar, coffee, and other commodities traveled from South America and the Caribbean to Spain by riding the northbound Gulf Stream until they reached Cape Hatteras and then turning east, catching the prevailing winds to cross the Atlantic. Spanish ships known for certain to have met disaster on the coast of North Carolina include *Nuestra de Solidad* at Drum Inlet and *El Salvador* at Topsail Inlet. At least two others ran aground between Currituck Inlet and Topsail Inlet in a storm in 1750 but managed to refloat themselves and continue on in a crippled condition. *Nuestra Señora de Guadalupe* crashed ashore at Ocracoke in that storm and was plundered by the locals, much to the consternation of colonial governor Gabriel Johnston.

As in the century before, in the 1700s European traders, especially the British, traveled north, via the Gulf Stream, along the Carolina coast before veering eastward for home ports across the Atlantic. The so-called "coastal trade"—that is, transporting cargoes north to south and south to north along the Atlantic coastline—also began flourishing in that century, and vessels involved in both that commerce and the overseas traffic went down off Diamond, Cape Lookout, and Frying Pan shoals and other dangerous points. In July 1770, for example, the *Glasgow Journal* reported: "There are several losses in North Carolina; among them one *Snow*, from Glasgow and one ship believed from London. The ship is totally lost and the *Snow* will lose all but some dry goods. The people were so lucky as to get into the pilot boats." The *Journal* also noted that "the ship *Lilly* . . . is lost going into North Carolina and considerable damage done to the goods." In that same year the *Edinburgh Evening Courant* reported that "the *Neptune* . . . from N. Carolina to London, sailed on the 4th of September last, being the day before the violent storm on that coast, and it is thought that all perished." In April 1771 the *Journal* observed that the *Rubie* in passage from Londonderry to North Carolina sank at Ocracoke bar. The *Virginia Gazette* of June 11, 1772, informed its readers that "in a gale of wind and weather, a schooner from Philadelphia, John Kerr master, bound for Portsmouth, deeply laden, was drove ashore at the mouth of Currituck Inlet, and beat to Pieces. The people were saved, but chief of the Cargo will be lost." On July 25, 1772, the *Courant* reported: "Captain Hunt, in the sloop *Sally*, from

New-York to Charles-Town, was cast away the 4th of May, on Cape Look-out shoals, 10 leagues from land; the vessel and cargo are entirely lost, with seven persons; the rest of the people, with much difficulty, got safe to shore, 15 in number; in the boat, after being in her 15 hours. The Captain was once knocked overboard, but with much difficulty was got in." On December 4, 1775, the same newspaper published this news: "The *Active* . . . is lost at North Carolina, all the crew perished." On December 9 the editor declared: "We learn from North Carolina, that the damage done by the late hurricane is incredible, the whole shore being lined with wrecks. Upwards of 100 dead bodies had drifted ashore at Occacock island." In May 1792 the insurance company Lloyds of London reported that the ship *Experiment*, traveling from North Carolina to New York, had been "lost on Cape Hatteras."

Despite the growing frequency and severity of such incidents, neither the colonial nor state and national governments (after the American Revolution) undertook to establish plans and policies for the rescue and aid of shipwreck victims. For many years land-based rescue on all coasts of the United States remained in large measure the responsibility of unorganized but humanitarian volunteers who spontaneously came to the assistance of those unfortunate persons who suffered shipping disasters. The nation's first organized service to provide aid to distressed vessels and their crews and passengers was the privately funded and operated Massachusetts Humane Society, founded in 1785. In 1791 the charter of the new society specified its mission: "The end and design of the institution is for the recovery of persons who meet with such accidents as to produce in them the appearance of death, and for promoting the cause of humanity by pursuing such means from time to time as shall have for their object the preservation of human life and the alleviation of its miseries." To fulfill its purpose the Massachusetts Humane Society constructed several boat-houses and houses of refuge (small huts providing shelter, food, and warmth for shipwrecked mariners) at points along that state's coastline that had proved dangerous to passing ships. It offered rewards to volunteers who participated in efforts to save and care for victims of shipping disasters. For the next two decades lifesaving operations remained the province of such humanitarian organizations as the Massachusetts society, although no others reached nearly the same proficiency as that one.

But in spite of its treacherous coastline and the large number of shipwrecks occurring there, North Carolina had no formal agency devoted to sea rescue. Without the help of organized, trained rescuers, many seamen simply drowned or otherwise lost their lives as a result of the calamities that occurred on the dreaded shoals of the Old North State. The crews and passengers of sloops, schooners, brigs, barks, steamers, and other craft that ran aground or became disabled off the Outer Banks frequently found that their escape from injury and death rested largely in their own hands. In 1733, for instance, the ship *Marget*, commanded by Richard Whistler and bound from Charleston to London, wrecked off Bodie Island. According to the *South Carolina Gazette*, "eleven Souls were drowned, among whom [were] Mrs. Westlid and her child, and Mrs. Howard's Daughter and another Girl, and 7 Men." The ship's mate reached shore safely. "He was knocked over board with the Yawl in the Breakers . . . and miraculously saved, and afterwards was the means of saving the others that stay'd 12 hours on the wreck, the Captain was the last he saved."

In 1800 the ever-increasing number of shipwrecks and lost cargoes led North Carolina to establish wreck districts with a commissioner or agent in charge of each of them to take possession of materials that washed ashore as the result of shipping disasters. Those officials, who initially were appointed by the governor and later by the county courts, attempted to determine the owner of the wrecked cargo and convened an auction, known as a vendue, for its disposition. According to the terms of vendue, the owner of the cargo, the person who salvaged it, and the agent all received a share of the selling price. In 1801 the state authorized the vendue masters (as the commissioners came to be called) to recruit or deputize coastal residents to assist in the rescue of shipwrecked sailors and passengers.

Although that was the first official attempt in North Carolina to enlist persons for rescue efforts, the self-sufficient, resourceful, and independent people of the Outer Banks often had risked their lives to save the lives of unknown mariners whom fate and dire circumstances had cast upon their shores. In the early days of settlement colonial officials had encouraged the inhabitation of the Banks by responsible and humanitarian people who would aid victims tossed ashore by wind and wave. In 1706 the colonial Council decreed "that the said Pleaces should not be settled by any straingers but what are of good fame, least any harme should befale any of her M's subjects that should through Chance be Cast away there."

But for the Bankers shipwrecks produced mixed feelings and motives. Salvaged cargoes provided them with materials, income, and sometimes even wealth. Lumber found adrift after wrecks went into the construction of houses in almost every village in coastal North Carolina. For generations the cry "Ship ashore!" or "Ship on beach!" sent locals madly scurrying to the shore to salvage what they could. Colonial governor Gabriel Johnston referred to the Outer Bankers as a "set of people who live on certain Sandy Islands lying between the Sound and the Ocean, and who are Wild and ungovernable, so that it is seldom possible to Execute any Civil or Criminal Writs among them." Those people, he claimed, "would come in a body and pillage the ships." Captain Albert I. Lewis, a onetime underwriters' agent, once remarked, "The people on Ocracoke and Hatteras would drop a corpse while carrying it to the grave, and leave it on the road, if they heard 'Ship on Beach!'" Still another resident remembered: "I have known when the signal is given, 'Ship on Beach,' crowds to leave church even during a revival meeting." During the colonial period the British government convicted and punished a number of coastal residents who removed equipment and property from the wrecks of ships belonging to the Crown. In February 1698, for example, the General Court of North Carolina tried several men who pillaged and attempted to destroy the wreck of the warship HMS *Swift Advice*, which had been "beat upon the sea shoar . . . by force of the Wind and Sea" at Currituck Inlet. The court sentenced two of the thieves to be "burnt in the brawn of the Left Thumb with a hott Iron having on it the Letter T." The court ordered a third defendant, an African American, to "be punished by receiving thirty one stripes on his bare back" for his role in permanently scuttling the *Swift Advice* by firing through her hull "with one great Gun."

Despite such attempts to punish and prevent coastal inhabitants from helping themselves to shipwreck cargoes, the isolation of the Outer Banks and the chaos surrounding shipping catastrophes generally made it possible, and even easy, for Bankers to avail themselves of those items that washed ashore. Even though they might do all in their power to save the life of a shipwreck victim and provide for his care, they did not necessarily extend the same courtesy to his possessions. In 1819 the captain of the sloop *Henry*, bound from New York to Charleston, experienced the dual attitude of Outer Bankers toward shipwrecks. The *Henry* ran aground on the south beach of Ocracoke bar, four miles from land. There she broke up and passengers and crew died. Although seriously injured, the captain survived, and he reported that he "received the kindest treatment, and every possible care from the inhabitants." He also noted, however: "My chest has been picked up, but it had been opened, and all my clothes of value taken out. I am here almost naked and shall try to get home as soon as I am able."

In addition to the efforts of local volunteers and those pressed into service by vendue masters, the keepers of North Carolina's lighthouses occasionally provided assistance and refuge to mariners who fell victim to wind and storm. In 1789 the federal

Before the establishment of formal lifesaving organizations, rescue of shipwrecked victims depended upon humane coastal residents who rushed to beaches to provide assistance. Engraving from *Harper's Weekly* (1877).

government took responsibility for building, maintaining, and staffing the lighthouses that marked dangerous spots along the new nation's coasts. By 1823 lighthouses stood at four of the most important points on the coast of the Old North State—Cape Hatteras, Ocracoke Inlet, Cape Lookout, and Cape Fear. In 1848 the federal government completed and staffed Bodie Island Lighthouse, south of Oregon Inlet. In subsequent years those five structures were upgraded or replaced as well as supplemented by such other navigational devices as lightships and beacons. The light towers warned seafarers away from the treacherous shoals that might claim their vessels and their lives. But the government intended lighthouses as aids to navigation. They were not built, equipped, or staffed as facilities for rescuing sailors victimized by angry seas.

In 1837 the United States government took its first official step toward aiding imperiled ships and other craft when Congress passed an act to allow the president "to cause any suitable number of public vessels adapted to the purpose, to cruise upon the coast, in the severe portion of the season, when the public service will allow it, and to afford such aid to distressed navigators as their circumstances and necessities may require; and such public vessels shall go to sea prepared fully to render such assistance." Although the act did not specify that the Revenue Marine Service should carry out its provisions, that organization immediately began using its cutters for rescue operations. But, as mentioned earlier, the Revenue Marine Service also had the responsibility for the enforcement of customs laws, a task that alone strained a sparsely manned and funded agency. In addition, the cutters had vast distances to patrol, and by the time one of them was summoned and finally arrived on the scene of a disaster, the worst had already happened. A system of providing lifesaving assistance from shore remained sorely needed. As early as 1838 the United States Senate Committee on Commerce began calling for a plan "to alleviate the distressed seamen by having lifeboats stationed at places . . .

designated." But not until 1847 did the federal government take specific steps to fund shore-based lifesaving capabilities. In that year Congress approved a motion by Congressman Robert McClelland of Michigan, chairman of the House Committee on Commerce, to add five thousand dollars for that purpose to the next year's lighthouse appropriation. Two years later the Department of the Treasury turned the money over to the collector of customs at Boston for the purchase of boathouses and various rescue devices at Cape Cod for the Massachusetts Humane Society. That step marked the national government's "first appropriation made for rendering assistance to the shipwrecked from the shore." Actual staffing and operations, however, still remained in the hands of private associations.

In 1848 Congress, at the behest of Congressman William A. Newell of New Jersey, passed a bill awarding to that state ten thousand dollars "for providing surf boats, rockets, cannonades, and other necessary apparatus for the better preservation of life and property from shipwrecks . . . between Sandy Hook and Little Egg Harbor." The Department of the Treasury designated an officer, Captain Douglas Ottinger, from the Revenue Marine Service to cooperate with the Board of Underwriters of New York to purchase boathouses and equipment for New Jersey. In the following year Congress dispensed another ten thousand dollars to extend the line of boathouses from Little Egg Harbor to Cape May and appropriated a like amount to establish stations on Long Island under the supervision of the Lifesaving Benevolent Association of New York.

During the next decade the federal government, acting through the Department of the Treasury, made a number of appropriations for facilities and equipment for lifesaving outposts on the coasts of Massachusetts, New Jersey, and Long Island and on the Great Lakes. Lifesaving efforts received a significant boost in 1854 when Congress passed an act "for the better preservation of life and property from vessels shipwrecked on the coasts of the United States." That statute empowered the secretary of the treasury to build new stations on the coasts of Long Island and New Jersey and to relocate, remove, and repair existing stations. It also provided for the appointment of a keeper at each station at a minimum annual salary of two hundred dollars, and it approved district superintendents for Long Island and New Jersey, who were to report to the secretary of the treasury. Under the law's provisions, lifeboats were placed under the care of United States officers or bonded persons in the neighborhood of a station, and stations at lighthouses became the responsibility of the lighthouse keepers.

The 1854 act was a milestone for the United States's lifesaving program because it ended the federal government's policy of merely providing funding and equipment to private persons or organizations, who then became responsible for organizing rescue crews and actually carrying out shore-based missions. After passing that law, the federal government took an operational role in lifesaving activity and brought to such efforts the important elements of supervision, continuity, and accountability. Before 1854, in the words of one treasury official, "There was no organization of any sort; no accounting to the Treasury for the property, or for anything that might happen or be done; no responsibility from anybody to anybody. There the buildings stood, many of them upon isolated portions of the coasts, far distant from any habitations, exposed to the malicious. As a matter of fact, upon the completion of the work, Captain Ottinger, as any careful man would have done under the circumstances, left the key of each boathouse with someone, probably suitable as he could find who would accept it, and left also with him a printed card of instructions as to the manner of using the articles." Yet, although the act of 1854 provided for the appointment of keepers to take permanent charge of lifesaving outposts, it failed to employ crews to man the stations. Keepers themselves may have been full-time officers, but they still had to round up volunteers to conduct rescue operations.

Furthermore, despite the marginal progress that the government made in supporting and advancing lifesaving activities before the Civil War (especially the 1854 legislation), it did not extend any substantial efforts beyond New Jersey, Long Island, Massachusetts, and the Great Lakes. In North Carolina rescues remained in the hands of vendue officials, local inhabitants, and lighthouse keepers, despite the ever-increasing number and severity of maritime disasters occurring in the waters off the state. At alarming rates, schooners, sloops, brigs, barks, and steamers continued to join the multitude of wrecks in the underwater graves of the dangerous Diamond Shoals and other perilous points along the coast.

For example, in February 1820 the brig *Sally*, returning to Wilmington from St. Thomas with a cargo of sugar, wrecked near New Topsail Inlet. Although the captain and crew survived, the vessel and cargo were lost. In March 1833 the line packet ship *William Drayton*, bound for Charleston from New York with a valuable cargo that included one hundred thousand dollars for the United States Bank, crashed ashore at Bodie Island. Fortunately, most of the cargo and specie were saved, and no one died in the accident. A gale in October drove ashore and destroyed at Bodie Island the brig *Hercules*, bound from Wilmington to New York. The same storm demolished the schooner *William*, owned by Outer Banker William Etheridge, off Cape Hatteras. Such ships as the *Horatio* (lost at Diamond Shoals in 1820 with eight crew members aboard) and the schooners *Enterprise, Emulous, Diomede, Harvest,* and *Victory* (all lost between New Inlet and Kitty Hawk, 1822-1825) also contributed to the number of Atlantic graveyard wrecks growing yearly in the first half of the nineteenth century. Almost every week a local newspaper in some North Carolina port published news of a shipping disaster in the waters of the state. On September 24, 1834, the *People's Press and Wilmington Advertiser* reported: "Sloop John Chevalier . . . from Charleston for this port, went ashore near Lockwood's Folly Inlet, on Thursday last, during the gale, and went to pieces—crew saved, and a part of the materials." On November 5 the same journal noted: "The Schr.

John McMullen from New York, for Elizabeth City, N.C. was totally lost on the night of the 12th ult. on Ocracoke Bar, crew saved, and part of the cargo in a damaged state."

One of North Carolina's worst shipping catastrophes occurred at Ocracoke in October 1837, when the steamboat *Home* (or *Volante Home*) fell victim to a hurricane, known as "Racer's Storm," that destroyed the ship and killed ninety passengers and crew. A new and elegantly designed passenger steamer out of New York, the *Home* was on only her third voyage when disaster struck. She had departed New York for Charleston on October 7, carrying a number of wealthy and prominent persons. The following evening she encountered the storm off the North Carolina coast and on the morning of the ninth suffered its full impact near Cape Hatteras. As the hurricane vented its fury, tremendous seas pummeled and tossed the packet so violently that her paddle wheels came completely out of the water. High seas began filling the hold, and the pumps could not work hard or fast enough to stay the flow. Passengers began bailing water with buckets and even pots and pans, anything that would hold water. Ultimately, Captain Carlton White decided to save the vessel by beaching her, and he ordered a westward course. In the afternoon the water in the hold finally extinguished the engine fires, and the vessel continued under sail until she ran aground about one hundred yards from the beach northeast of Ocracoke Village around 10:00 P.M. There it seemed the violent storm would literally beat the *Home* to pieces. In a state of panic, crew and passengers rushed for the lifeboats. Unfortunately, one lifeboat already had been crushed, and the storm splintered another when the crew attempted to launch it. The third lifeboat, filled with people, was lowered over the side but almost immediately capsized in the waves. The *Home* had only two life preservers aboard, and those were commandeered by two men who eventually reached shore safely.

As wind and waves lashed the grounded steamer, the women and children passengers huddled together on the forecastle.

Victims aboard the passenger steamer *Home*, which wrecked at Ocracoke in 1837. Photograph of engraving from North Carolina Collection, University of North Carolina Library, Chapel Hill.

But suddenly that portion of the ship broke away, spilling them into the boiling surf, where most of them perished. Under the constant pounding of the storm, the *Home* soon disintegrated into three pieces, casting her remaining occupants into the merciless and violently raging sea. Of the 130 men, women, and children aboard, only 40 survived. The residents of Ocracoke rendered what rescue assistance they could and cared for the survivors. On the morning of October 10, 1837, bodies and wreckage littered the beach. A century later T. W. Howard of Ocracoke recalled his grandmother's telling him that on the morning following the "heartbreaking" disaster she viewed "bodies clad in broadcloth and silk, women and men cold in death bedecked with diamonds and costly jewels lying on the beach for miles among or amid the debris."

Pilot boats and other rescue craft brought the survivors to Wilmington, where they received care before leaving for home. The news of their plight sparked the emotions of the citizens of Wilmington. "Youth, age, and infancy," lamented the *People's Press* of the port city, "have been cut off in a single night, and found a common death under the same billow. . . . We have never seen a deeper sensation pervade our community than the reception of this intelligence has produced. The profoundest sympathy is engraved on every countenance, and all wear the aspect of those sorrowing for their own dead. We feel assured that all feel an anxious solicitude to alleviate the distress of those unfortunate survivors who may come among us, and vehicles have already been sent out to bring them into our town, and provision made for their reception."

In less than a year after the *Home* calamity another luxury passenger steamer, the *Pulaski*, recently constructed in Baltimore and bound from Charleston with 155 passengers aboard, wrecked near New River Inlet. The *Pulaski*'s boiler exploded after the steamer rounded Cape Fear in mid-June 1838, killing a number of persons immediately. As the ship broke apart other passengers and crew were killed or drowned, and five perished when two lifeboats overturned in the surf. Some survived aboard rafts that drifted for days before a schooner came to their rescue. Others clung to wreckage until they were picked up or washed ashore, and six men managed to reach safety in a deck boat. But in the final count one hundred men, women, and children had died in the disaster.

Calamities involving smaller craft, sometimes used for pleasure, contributed to the death toll in North Carolina waters. In a "melancholy disaster" of August 1833, for example, a sailboat piloted by a Colonel Dozier on an outing from the "neighborhood of Smithville [Southport] to the Banks" capsized at the mouth of the Cape Fear River with nineteen persons—mostly women and children—aboard. Twelve drowned and the remaining seven "were two hours in the water" before help arrived. A slave named Fortune belonging to Colonel Dozier's brother, John, rescued the survivors. "We trust that his great exertions, in the exercise of duty will not go unrewarded," proclaimed the *People's Press*.

The terrible storms of July and August 1842 resulted in an incredible loss of shipping and people. The first hurricane of that season struck Cape Hatteras on the afternoon of July 12, and it proved to be one of the most destructive ever to hit the coast. Losses of lives and property were reported all the way from Norfolk, Virginia, to Cape Lookout, and the center of the storm apparently passed over Ocracoke and Portsmouth islands. Off Hatteras the schooner *Lexington* was hit hard, and the captain and crew abandoned ship. Off Diamond Shoals, huge breakers capsized and pulverized two unknown ships. Their entire crews were lost, and seven local men who tried to salvage the cargoes also perished. Fourteen vessels ran ashore between New Inlet and Ocracoke Island. The storm swept still another six out to sea from Ocracoke Inlet, and those were presumed lost.

Outer Bankers had only begun to recover from the July hurricane when another storm struck on August 24. That one destroyed three known vessels, ran aground a number of others, and killed at least eight sailors. The brig *Kilgore*, traveling from Trinidad to Baltimore, ran ashore on Currituck Beach, but her crew survived. The brig *Pioneer*, heading for Norfolk with a load of salt from Turks Island in the Bahamas, crashed ashore on Ocracoke Island and lost one crew member. The ship *Congress*, also carrying Turks Island salt, wrecked on Cape Hatteras and seven persons died.

Every year brought more wholesale death and destruction as seagoing craft of various shapes and sizes continued to fall victim to the happenstance of wind, storm, and wave and joined the many other ill-fated vessels in the Graveyard of the Atlantic. In 1845 the French bark *Emilie* left Bordeaux and crossed the Atlantic for Norfolk. She had no trouble until her captain, besieged by bad weather, misjudged the light at Cape Henry, Virginia, and the vessel ran aground. She instantly sank in two fathoms of water near the boundary between North Carolina and Virginia. With no rescue assistance forthcoming from shore (only 150 yards away), the ten-man crew of the *Emilie* attempted to launch the ship's lifeboat, but it broke up and sank. The sailors then sought safety in the rigging as the storm and spray pounded them throughout the night. The next day one man tried to swim ashore but drowned. Six others attempted to build a raft but were washed from the bark into the breakers and drowned. After the storm local residents found only three of the Frenchmen still alive, one of whom was near death.

One of North Carolina's maritime catastrophes even resulted in cannibalism. When the bark *Orline St. John*, out of Norfolk for Barbados, wrecked in a severe gale off Hatteras, the survivors remained in the rigging for a full week without food or water. Finally they were reduced to eating the body of a sailor named Douglass, who had died from exposure.

A count made from David Stick's compilation of shipwrecks reveals that at least 128 verifiable vessels became complete losses on the North Carolina coast between 1526 and 1860. In the decade 1850-1860 alone, approximately forty-one verified vessels were totally lost. Such tragedies were vivid and shocking reminders to coastal North Carolinians and to federal officials of the pressing need for a government-funded and -supervised rescue service. By the mid-nineteenth century the fact had grown painfully obvious that North Carolina and, indeed, all of the coastal United States desperately needed a well-regulated force, staffed by trained men of extraordinary courage and nautical skill, to deal with the ever-growing number of ship disasters.

But suddenly and regrettably the federal effort to expand the nation's lifesaving operations—theretofore a slow process at best—came to a complete standstill as a result of the outbreak of the Civil War. "Under the pressures of the Civil War," writes one authority, Howard V. L. Bloomfield, "life-saving was forgotten. All that remained of the system by 1870 were some weather-beaten huts serving as headquarters for keepers who had little or nothing to keep." Lifeboats became ruined by neglect. In New Jersey one of them was "carted around the neighborhood to be used as a trough for mixing mortar or as a scalding tub at hog-killing time."

During the war United States ships had to pass North Carolina's treacherous capes to convey troops and supplies to war zones in the South. After Union expeditions captured Hatteras Island in August 1861 and Roanoke Island in February 1862, much of coastal North Carolina remained in Federal hands for the rest of the conflict. As a result, a number of United States transports, gunboats, and other vessels sank in the state's waters, because of either combat or the notorious violent storms that plagued the coast. In mid-January 1862, as General Ambrose E. Burnside marshaled his naval and land forces to attack Roanoke Island, several of his ships sank or stranded in a storm near Hatteras Inlet. The steamer *City of New York* struck the beach and was "lashed to pieces by the angry waves," and the *Zouave* also went to the bottom at the inlet. The *Pocahontas*, an old and unseaworthy ship carrying

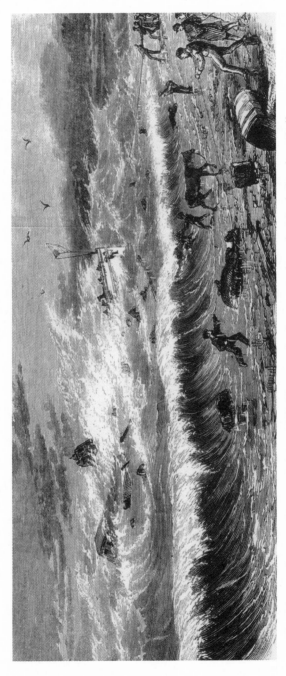

Wreck of the *Pocahontas* at Hatteras Inlet in 1862. Photograph of engraving from the North Carolina Collection.

at least seventy-five horses belonging to two Rhode Island regiments, wrecked near Kinnakeet. The fifty men aboard and thirty horses were rescued but the ship sank. Subsequent reports claimed that the captain and engineer had been drunk since their departure from Rhode Island. The best-known ship to wreck off the North Carolina coast during the war was the famous Union ironclad *Monitor*, which sank in a storm off Cape Hatteras in December 1862. There she still rests, bottom up, in 220 feet of water. A number of Confederate blockade-runners, privateers, and gunboats also went down in Tar Heel waters. But all rescue efforts, by either side, remained spontaneous and improvised.

Although the Civil War halted all official lifesaving operations throughout the states, the postwar period soon brought renewed and intensified interest in protecting and assisting maritime trade. The demands of a wartime economy had added an impetus to the Industrial Revolution that began moving the nation away from its simple, agrarian beginnings and toward the complicated, industrialized twentieth century. Beginning in the 1870s, the transportation of goods and raw materials by seagoing conveyances, as well as overland by rail, swelled as part of the new industrial and commercial boom in late-nineteenth-century America.

To meet the pressing need to safeguard the country's growing maritime traffic, the federal government launched a two-part program. It began building a series of lighthouses having powerful lights and constructed close enough together to give ships continual guidance as they traveled the north-south route of the Atlantic. On the North Carolina coast the government constructed new brick lighthouses at Cape Hatteras (1870); Bodie Island (1872), north of Oregon Inlet; and Currituck Beach (1875). Those structures followed the modern design of the new Cape Lookout Lighthouse, which had replaced the old one in 1859. The new and distinctive towers came under the jurisdiction of the

The famous ironclad *Monitor* (*foreground*) sank off Cape Hatteras in December 1862. The steamer *Rhode Island* (*background*) rescued a number of the crew. Engraving from *Harper's Weekly* (1863).

Lighthouse Board, a division—established on the eve of the Civil War—of the United States Department of the Treasury.

The other part of the government's effort to protect and assist the sailors and cargoes of the growing shipping industry was the official creation of the United States Lifesaving Service. In 1870 Congress appropriated money to hire experienced six-man surfboat crews at alternating lifesaving stations on the New Jersey coast. The following year the secretary of the treasury appointed Sumner I. Kimball as chief of the Revenue Marine Service, and Kimball immediately began an inspection of the lifesaving stations in New Jersey and Long Island. There he discovered "a number of rude huts, each containing a boat such as was used by the local fishermen in passing through the surf, and a few articles of primitive apparatus for use in efforts to effect rescue from vessels which might be wrecked in the vicinity." As a result of Kimball's findings, Congress passed a number of appropriations (totaling two hundred thousand dollars) to establish the United States Lifesaving Service as a branch under the supervision of the Revenue Marine Service and to extend the system of lifesaving stations to states that did not already have them. It also allowed for the staffing of the stations with experienced surfmen, who were to be paid a maximum of forty-six dollars per month. Those measures authorized for the first time the ending of the "volunteer" aspect of the United States's lifesaving activities and the substitution of a system directly and entirely controlled by the federal government.

To create an official lifesaving division, the Revenue Marine Service reorganized its personnel; restored existing stations and equipment; established beach patrols and signals, rules for governing the new branch, and regular procedures for inspections; and made provisions for awarding lifesaving medals. Kimball launched an international search for the best equipment, and he demonstrated considerable administrative skill in setting up the organization. Much of the service's subsequent success can be attributed to his conscientious efforts. In 1872 Congress approved stations at Cape Cod and Block Island, Rhode Island. An act of 1873 provided for the creation of stations on the coasts of Maine, New Hampshire, northern Massachusetts, Virginia, and finally North Carolina. Legislation of the following year made provision for stations for Delaware, Maryland, Virginia (additional), Florida, the Great Lakes, and the Pacific coast. To oversee the activities of those facilities, the Revenue Marine Service divided them among twelve lifesaving districts and appointed a superintendent to be in charge of each district. North Carolina and southern Virginia comprised Lifesaving District No. 6. "Colonel" Charles Guirkin of Elizabeth City became the first superintendent of that district.

Construction of stations on the Outer Banks began early in 1874. On April 15 the Elizabeth City *North Carolinian* reported that buildings at Kitty Hawk, Bodie Island, Chicamacomico, and Little Kinnakeet were "in process of erection or marked out." Equipment also began arriving. "A number of the surf boats belonging to the Life Saving Service has been lying at our wharf the past week," reported the same newspaper on December 9. By the end of the year seven stations stood on the Banks: Jones Hill (later called Whales Head and Currituck Beach), Caffeys Inlet, Kitty Hawk, Nags Head, Bodie Island (located south of Oregon Inlet and later named Oregon Inlet Station), Chicamacomico, and Little Kinnakeet. The completion of those new, freshly painted but lonely outposts marked the beginning of one of the most heroic and humanitarian eras in North Carolina's past.

Chapter 2
Buildings, Men, and Equipment

As originally constructed, the lifesaving stations of coastal North Carolina were basic, utilitarian structures. Local contractors and workmen built the facilities according to federal specifications. In general, the North Carolina buildings featured the same design as the other fifteen stations built throughout the nation in 1874, and they contrasted to a considerable extent with the "plain, barnlike buildings" that preceded them along the northern coastline. Cognizant of the rough environment in which the outposts had to stand, the builders constructed them of pine weatherboards with cypress or cedar shingles and upon posts of cypress or locust wood. Adorned with decorative board-and-batten and king-post ornaments, the structures "displayed a new attention to architectural image" in a cottage style, belonging to a broader design mode known as Picturesque.

Each of the first stations was a steep-gabled two-story house measuring 18 to 20 feet wide by 40 feet long. (The dimensions soon changed to 20 feet by 45 feet.) An open watchtower capped the roof. Two rooms occupied the ground floor. One of those, the boat room, took two-thirds of the lower level and

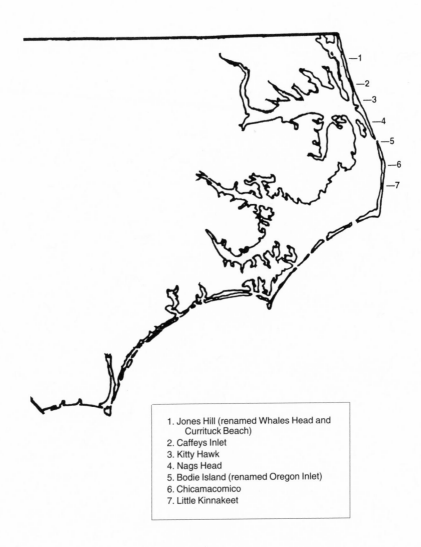

1. Jones Hill (renamed Whales Head and Currituck Beach)
2. Caffeys Inlet
3. Kitty Hawk
4. Nags Head
5. Bodie Island (renamed Oregon Inlet)
6. Chicamacomico
7. Little Kinnakeet

NORTH CAROLINA STATIONS BUILT 1874

contained such heavy equipment as a lifeboat, mounted on a four-wheel carriage, a life car, ropes and hawsers, and a two-wheel "beach apparatus" cart containing various implements for effecting rescues from the shore. The crew entered and exited the boat room by a large double door, in front of which was a wooden ramp to facilitate rolling the lifeboat and the beach apparatus out of the building and onto the beach. The remaining one-third of the first floor functioned as a type of living room for the lifesavers, where they also prepared their meals. Cisterns and shallow wells supplied water, and all the stations had outdoor toilets. Supplies for the original seven outposts arrived by boat from Elizabeth City.

The second floor had three rooms, one of which held equipment, records and books, and a first aid cabinet. One of the remaining rooms, with cots, served as sleeping quarters for the crew and any shipwreck victims. The commander, called the keeper, occupied the third room as his quarters.

In addition to its regular stations, the Lifesaving Service maintained lifeboat stations (smaller structures containing an additional lifeboat and equipment) and houses of refuge for the temporary care of wreck victims. North Carolina may have had one lifeboat station on Hatteras Island but had no houses of refuge. Victims were cared for at the stations or sometimes housed in local homes.

Originally, six crewmen, called surfmen, and a keeper made up the staff at each of the lifesaving stations. Each surfman had to be at least eighteen years old and physically fit. The Lifesaving Service filled its ranks with men who were residents of the areas in which they served, usually experienced fishermen or other types of mariners familiar with local weather, tides, currents, and topographical conditions. Many coastal families served for generations as lifesavers. Any account of the heroic exploits of the North Carolina service includes a list of such well-known coastal Carolina names as Midgett, Meekins, Pugh, Gray, and Etheridge.

Keepers had extensive experience afloat and in handling men and equipment. They held responsibility for the management of the stations and the training and discipline of the crews. They kept a daily log or journal and each month sent a transcript to their district superintendent. They led the surfmen on all rescue attempts, gave all commands, and took the steering oar when the lifeboat was used. The earliest keepers of North Carolina's first seven stations were John G. Gale (Jones Hill); W. G. Partridge (Caffeys Inlet); W. D. Tate (Kitty Hawk); John W. Evans (Nags Head); Edward Drinkwater (Bodie Island); Benjamin S. Pugh (Chicamacomico); and Banister Midgett (Little Kinnakeet).

Although keepers remained employed year-round at an annual salary in 1874 of two hundred dollars, surfmen in the beginning manned the stations only in the "active" season during the winter months December through March. While on active duty they received a salary of forty dollars per month. But even in the inactive season, surfmen could be summoned to duty in the event of a shipwreck. For their services on such occasions they received three dollars each. Surfmen were ranked and numbered according to experience and competence, and each one had specific tasks during operations. Surfman no. 1 stood second in command to the keeper and took his place if he became incapacitated.

Within a short time after their establishment, the lifesaving stations of North Carolina were systematically deploying standardized equipment and rescue procedures as specified by Revenue Marine chief Kimball. In the active season surfmen at each station kept a proper watch at all hours. During the day when the weather remained clear, a stationary lookout maintained a watch in the tower. The lookout focused sharp eyes on ocean and sounds and usually kept a record of vessels passing along the coastline. He also used signal flags to signal other stations or to inform ships of dangerous shoals and weather or their correct longitude and latitude. Telegraph lines soon connected the stations to each other and to headquarters in Washington. Telephone

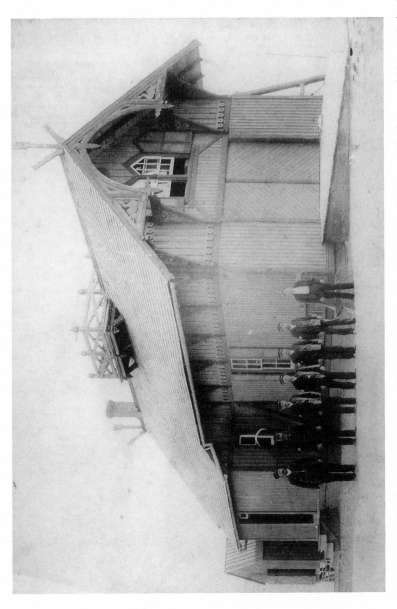

Nags Head (*top*) and Little Kinnakeet stations. Photographs from State Archives, Division of Archives and History, Raleigh.

Warning a vessel away from shore. Engraving from *Harper's Weekly* (1888).

lines followed after they were first introduced between some New Jersey stations in 1884. At night—or sometimes in daylight, when the weather was bad and visibility poor—two lookouts from each station walked the beach patrol. The night duty was divided into four watches: sunset to 8:00 P.M.; 8:00 P.M. to midnight; midnight to 4:00 A.M.; and 4:00 A.M. to sunrise. When a watch began the lookouts departed the station in opposite directions and traveled along the surf line to a prescribed point before returning to their base. By the time all twenty-nine stations were completed on the Tar Heel coast, the outposts stood in most cases about 5 to 7 miles apart. Thus each beach patroller covered between 2½ and 3½ miles before reaching halfway the distance to the next station. At that point he entered a "half-way house," or shed, where he exchanged "checks," or tokens, with the beach lookout from the adjacent station, thereby verifying on his return to his own that he had performed his assignment. Patrollers from isolated stations

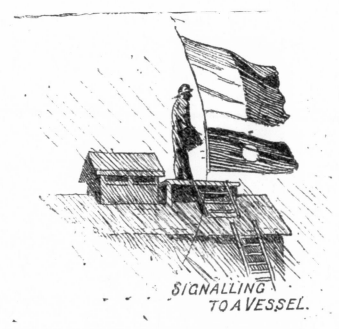

Signaling with flags. Engraving from *Harper's Weekly* (1888).

carried a time clock, activated by a key kept at a halfway house at the end of their beat. Lifesaving regulations specified that "failure to maintain the patrol [is] always in this service, like unfaithfulness in the guard of the soldier, unpardonable" and that "the duty of maintaining vigilant and unremitting watch upon the coast is paramount and absolute."

Each surfman walking the beach patrol carried a lantern and several red Coston lights (signal flares). Sometimes he used those flares to warn ships away from the beach or shoals where they might run aground. If he witnessed or discovered a wreck, he immediately lighted a Coston light, which ignited into a brilliant flame. The flare notified the crew of the disabled vessel that they had been sighted and help was on the way. The Lifesaving Service published instructions to sailors that "if your vessel is stranded through the night and discovered by the patrolman, which you will know by his burning a brilliant red light, keep a bright lookout for signs of the arrival of the life-saving crew abreast of your vessel."

The majority of ships that wrecked off the North Carolina coast ran aground and wrecked close to shore—usually within a few hundred yards. That was true primarily because, before the advent of such modern equipment as diesel engines, sophisticated navigational devices, and ship-to-shore radio, ships involved in the Atlantic coast trade avoided the open seas and hugged the coastline as they traveled north and south. Moreover, northbound ships could ride the four-mile-an-hour current of the Gulf Stream that passed so close to Cape Hatteras. Those heading south could avoid bucking the current by traveling out several hundred miles beyond the stream before resuming the southward trip. Or they could save valuable time by sailing directly down the coast between the Gulf Stream and the Outer Banks. Of course, those who chose the latter alternative ran the risk of being wrecked upon the dangerous shoals. For many of them that is exactly what happened—especially if storms struck while they attempted to navigate the treacherous North Carolina capes. Because such hapless vessels struck hard aground close to the beach and remained lodged there, or were beached near shore by their captains, most took some time to break apart even in the worst conditions; very few went down suddenly in a *Titanic*-like fashion.

Nevertheless, many sailors and passengers died when they tried to save themselves by abandoning ship. The Lifesaving Service therefore stressed that the wrecked mariners should stay aboard their grounded vessel if possible and await the arrival of the lifesavers. The service's instructions further emphasized: "From one to four hours may intervene between the business of the [Coston] light and their arrival, as the patrolman may have to return to his station." Once back at his headquarters, the beach patrolman alerted the keeper and the rest of the surfmen as to the circumstances of the disaster. At that point, the keeper decided on the method of rescue.

If the surf was dangerously high and the wreck was within the range in which the surfmen could fire rescue lines from the shore, the keeper called for the deployment of the so-called beach apparatus. That apparatus included a number of pieces of equipment, all contained in a two-wheel cart pulled by the surfmen (eventually by a pony or horse) to a site parallel to the grounded vessel. Straining with the cart through sand and setting up the apparatus, usually in violent weather, required considerable stamina, strength, and skill from a crew. Frequent drills kept the men in readiness. The equipment in the beach apparatus cart consisted of ropes and pulleys; a sand anchor; a small cannon or mortar for firing lines; a wooden frame or prop called a crotch; a breeches buoy, which was a life ring with canvas trouser legs; and a "faking box," which held coiled lines free from tangles.

At the site of the wreck the surfmen skillfully and rapidly began their preassigned duties in deploying the equipment for the rescue of the shipwrecked sailors. Two men set and charged the gun to fire lines out to the ship. Two others assembled the sand anchor and began digging a pit in which to bury it. The final pair prepared the necessary lines and attached the breeches buoy to a three-inch hawser.

The beach apparatus cart. Engraving from *Harper's Weekly* (1888).

The keeper then fired the gun loaded with a weight attached to the end of a line, called the shot line, coiled in the faking box. In firing the shot line to the stricken craft, the lifesavers aimed for the rigging and tried to keep the shot to the windward, hoping that the line would be blown to the wreck even if the weight missed the rigging. The imperiled sailors seized the shot line and hauled it in, finding connected to it a pulley called a tail block with a "whip," or endless line, pulled through it. Tied to the whip was a "tally board," or wooden tablet, with printed instructions in English and French telling the victims to attach the block to a mast or other stable object. The surfmen then tied the hawser on the whip and drew it to the vessel, where the men on board made it fast to the mast about two feet above the tail block. After that was accomplished, the surfmen tied their end of the hawser to the double pulley of the sand anchor and placed the X-shaped crotch under the hawser to raise it above the waves and rough seas. Having buried the sand anchor, they pulled the hawser taut using the double pulley.

The breeches buoy hung from the hawser by means of a free-running block known as a traveler block. Using the whip line attached to the traveler block and to the tail block aboard the ship,

Firing the shot line. Engraving from *Harper's Weekly* (1888).

the surfmen pulled the breeches buoy out to the wreck. One at a time the victims saved themselves by sitting in the trouser legs of the buoy and allowing the crew on the beach to draw them ashore. "In many instances," the service instructed mariners, "two men can be landed in the breeches buoy at the same time, by each putting a leg through a leg of the breeches and holding on to the lifts of the buoy." Captains were to ensure that women and children landed first and that the latter "should be in the arms of elder persons or securely lashed to the buoy." Occasionally, in lieu of the breeches buoy, the lifesavers may have dispatched a "life car," which could rescue a larger number of persons—usually four to six—at one time. Constructed of metal, the cone-shaped life car, used in the United States since 1849, resembled a covered boat, with a hatch through which passengers entered. North Carolina's surfmen, however, seldom used the life car. It was heavy and clumsy and required a stouter hawser than the breeches buoy. The buoy proved faster and generally more practical and efficient than the car, and, in fact, virtually replaced the life car throughout the service after Kimball adopted it as standard equipment in 1872. In dire circumstances in which a ship seemed about to break apart, the lifesavers, in the interest of saving time, dispensed with the hawser and simply sent the breeches buoy out to the wreck on the whip line and drew the victims to shore directly through the surf.

The crews of the Lifesaving Service made their most daring rescues by using lifeboats. The lifeboats most commonly used by North Carolina lifesavers were known as surfboats. The boats varied slightly in design from area to area but had the same basic configuration. They generally were constructed of white cedar with white oak frames. (Before the Civil War some lifesaving boats had been made of metal by the New York company of inventor Joseph Francis, the same firm that manufactured the life car.) Their dimensions were 25 to 27 feet in length and 6½ to 7 feet in width. They had little keel and drew about six to seven feet of water. They weighed from seven hundred to eleven hundred

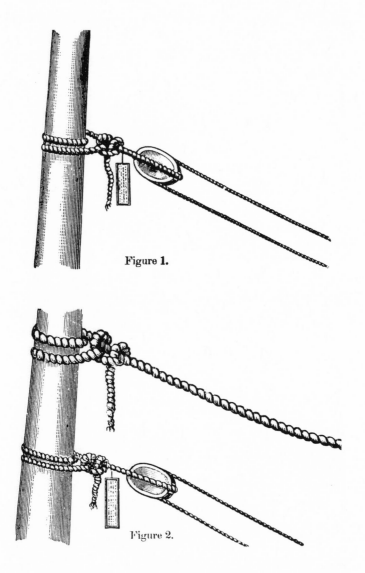

Figure **1.**

Figure 2.

Above and adjacent page: Attaching whip line and hawser to the mast of a distressed ship to effect a rescue with breeches buoy. Engravings from *Annual Report of the Operations of the United States Lifesaving Service* (1900).

pounds, and each contained an air chamber, as well as cork around the gunwales, for buoyancy. A surfboat could carry from ten to twelve persons besides the crew, but in particularly perilous situations the lifesavers dangerously overloaded them, even in rough seas. Lifesavers also used another type of craft, heavier and longer, called simply "lifeboats." Those craft, which originally were thirty-four but after 1908 thirty-six feet in length, did not launch easily into the surf because of their size and weight. Consequently they were utilized primarily at stations located on the calm waters of inlets, bays, and rivers. Some surfboats and lifeboats ultimately had self-bailing capabilities. During most of the existence of the Lifesaving Service, oars, and occasionally sails, remained the only means of powering both types of boats, for before the perfection of the internal combustion engine, steam engines were too cumbersome to be effective. Surfmen referred to rowing as using "armstrong engines," and over the years they demonstrated considerable physical prowess by rowing for long periods in rough water to save the lives of many ill-fated sailors.

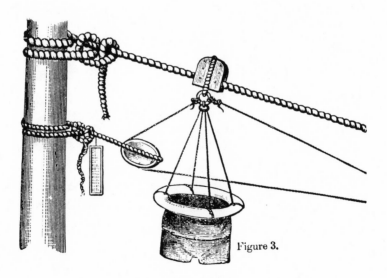

Figure 3.

Rescue with breeches buoy as depicted by American painter Winslow Homer in *The Lifeline* (1884). Philadelphia Museum of Art: The George W. Elkins Collection.

RESCUE WITH
BUOY AND HAWSER

Pulling victim ashore. Engraving from *Harper's Weekly* (1888).

The men of the Lifesaving Service employed the boats when wrecks occurred out of range of the gun (generally about five hundred yards) from the beach apparatus and the conditions of the surf made it possible to launch them. When a keeper had determined to use a surfboat in a rescue operation, the surfmen (but later horses) pulled the boat, mounted on the four-wheel carriage, to the scene of the disaster. There the crew unloaded the craft from the cart and began the difficult task of getting it into the surf and beyond the breakers. The men waded out with the boat, and some of them held it steady while others clamored in. Once under way, as the crew pulled on the oars, the keeper steered from the stern with the steering oar.

Long hours and backbreaking labor at the oars frequently lay ahead of the lifesavers as they began their mission of mercy. Heavy, pounding waves, currents, and violent wind and rain could combine to make their sorties difficult and life threatening.

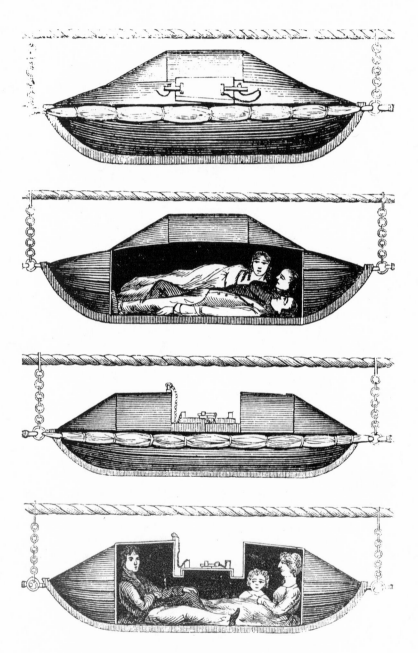

Life cars. Engravings from *Harper's New Monthly Magazine* (1851).

Rescue with life car. Engraving from *Harper's New Monthly Magazine* (1851).

Seemingly endless, exhausting periods of time and effort might pass before they returned safely to the beach with their human cargo of survivors. On many occasions a crew had to row miles to effect a rescue and then negotiate boat-smashing surf and treacherous undertows as they tried to beach their boat.

During operations with a boat the keeper possessed full authority over everyone involved, including the captain of the distressed vessel. The service's instructions to captains read:

Upon the boat reaching your vessel the directions and orders of the keeper (who always commands and steers the boat) should be implicitly obeyed. Any headlong rushing and crowding should be prevented, and the captain of the vessel should remain on board to preserve order until every person has left.

Women, children, helpless persons, and passengers should be passed into the boat first.

Goods or baggage will not be taken into the boat under any circumstances until all persons are landed. If any be passed in against the keeper's remonstrance he is fully authorized to throw it overboard.

In addition to their rescue duties, the North Carolina lifesavers saved thousands of dollars worth of property over the

Pulling surfboat to beach. Engraving from *Harper's Weekly* (1888).

Launching (*top*) and beaching surfboat. Engravings from *Harper's Weekly* (1888).

years. They helped to refloat vessels that had stranded on bars in either ocean or sounds. They also took custody of cargo that washed ashore until a vendue could be held for its disposition. Sometimes they recovered bodies that mysteriously washed ashore, with no indication of the circumstances leading to the fate of the victims. In December 1878, for example, Keeper Benjamin Pugh reported that "on Wednesday, Dec 11, a man washed ashore on Chica-macomico beach . . . supposed to be a sailor, drowned from some vessel. Young man, very stout, weight about 180 pounds, light sandy hair. Height 6 ft. Had no clothes but shirt and drawers. Had on a belt and sheaf. I had him shrouded, and a box made and had him buried."

Regardless of how proficient the surfmen became with beach apparatus or surfboat, seldom did a ship disaster unfold in such a way as to permit the lifesavers to conduct a rescue entirely according to the officially prescribed procedure. Nature and fate nearly always intervened to complicate and hinder operations, often to the point that keepers and men were stretched to their mental and physical limits to save the lives of mariners who certainly would have perished without their aid.

Eventually the Lifesaving Service specified the daily duties and training to be performed uniformly at all its stations. On Monday surfmen cleaned their station and repaired and polished their equipment. On Tuesday they drilled with the surfboat. They practiced with the signal flags on Wednesday and devoted Thursday to drill with the beach apparatus and breeches buoy. On Friday the lifesavers practiced first aid and methods of resuscitating victims. Saturday was the day for laundry and personal gear and Sunday for rest and religious services. Usually crew members took turns preparing meals, but at times the government employed cooks (both male and female) for the stations. Surfmen received one weekday per week for visiting with their families living nearby.

By the time the Lifesaving Service was fully operational on the coast of North Carolina, the Tar Heel surfmen had demonstrated time and again their courage and professionalism in saving lives. But before it could completely prove the skill, daring, and devotion to duty of its crews, the North Carolina service itself fell victim to charges of incompetence and political favoritism. Almost from the outset it became embroiled in controversy over the competency of its keepers and surfmen.

In the 1875-1876 season, amid public claims that some unqualified lifesavers were given their jobs solely for political and patronage reasons, a federal board visited District No. 6 and examined the keepers and surfmen at the seven North Carolina and three Virginia stations in the district. Of the seventy-nine keepers and surfmen, the board approved sixty-four and dismissed fifteen, four of whom were keepers. Two of the latter had "no knowledge whatever" of their duties, one lacked experience as a surfman, and the fourth was physically unqualified. Among the eleven surfmen rejected, five had no experience in using boats, three were physically unfit, two were the son and brother respectively of a keeper, and one was insubordinate. The board reported that the relieved men had been replaced but that the poor pay offered by the service made it difficult to obtain qualified keepers.

In its report of 1876-1877, the board observed that the lifesavers of District No. 6 had been demoralized by the "temporary control of its affairs gained by petty local politicians, whose aim was to subordinate the service to their personal ends; their method being to endeavor to pack the stations with their own creatures, without the slightest respect to use or competency." Alarmed by the impact of political favoritism, the board continued its tirade against such appointments in the district. "The success of these measures," the report declared, "would at once involve the utter ruin of the service; for what stranded crew, clinging to the shrouds of a vessel going to pieces in the breakers, could hope for succor in the hour of their bitter extremity, from life-saving stations recruited from the cross-roads grocery? It would be indeed an evil day when the wrecked sea-farer could look for help only to the puppets of local politics, where once his reliance was upon the heroic groups of tried surfmen." The board asserted that it had no evidence that rewards of positions in the service involved party politics at the state or national level. "But, considering the criminal mischief and disaster their success would involve, they acquire a deeper baseness from the circumstances of their having been invariably resorted to for no better purpose than to further the election of some local nobody to an office of no higher dignity than that of town constable or pound keeper."

About the same time as the board's investigation the first superintendent of District No. 6, Charles Guirkin, relinquished his position after only a short time in office. Guirkin, a prominent member of the Elizabeth City banking house of Guirkin and Company, a former town commissioner, and subsequently post-master, apparently had no lifesaving or maritime expertise. Guirkin's replacement, John J. Guthrie, however, brought to the superintendency considerable experience at sea. He had served as a naval officer in the Coast Survey and Observatory and on men-of-war in the Mediterranean, the Spanish Main, the East and West Indies, and off the coast of Africa. He also spoke several languages, and he labored to improve conditions within his new command. "The superintendent of this district," reported the board, "has been indefatigable in his efforts to perfect the discipline and efficiency of the stations under his charge." Guthrie would lose his life in the line of duty in 1877.

The service's annual report of 1876-1877 concluded that the recent replacement of incompetents had nullified the favor-itism and injurious impact of local politicians, that discipline and efficiency had been improved, and that the sixth district stood ready to perform as well as any other. Eventually the service set high standards for the selection of superintendents by mandating that "superintendents must not be less than 25 nor more than 55 years of age; be able to read and write the English language; and be familiar with the line of coast embraced in their districts and conversant with the management of surfboats, lifeboats, and life-saving apparatus and appliances in general use at life-saving sta-tions. They are appointed after competitive examinations, in which the keepers participate. The general superintendent selects one of the three highest of those who pass, and such candidate is appointed by the Secretary of the Treasury."

Keepers received appointments on the joint recommen-dation of the assistant inspector of the service and the district superintendent. Each keeper had to be a "man of character, phy-sique, and skill," as well as a surfman. Ultimately, superintendents and keepers selected their surfmen from registers of eligible men furnished by the Civil Service Commission. Accusations of political favoritism, however, would plague the Lifesaving Service for the rest of its existence.

Like political meddling, a lack of experience and training continued to trouble the Lifesaving Service during its early career in North Carolina. That lack of experience and training was at least partly responsible for the disaster that befell the entire Jones Hill crew during a rescue attempt at Currituck Beach in March 1876. Shortly after nightfall on the first of that month, the Italian bark *Nuova Ottavia* ran aground on a bar just north of the Jones Hill station. Keeper John G. Gale ordered out five of his men (the sixth having been sent for supplies)—Spencer Gray, Lemuel Griggs, Lewis White, Malachi Brumsey, and Jerry Munden—and they pulled their surfboat from the station to the beach. There a bystander, George W. Wilson, volunteered to replace the missing surfman, and the crew began rowing to the stranded bark in a rough sea. It is not clear whether it was because of inexperience or of darkness or other conditions that keeper Gale chose to use the lifeboat instead of the beach apparatus. The wreck was, after all, well within range of the mortar, and the cart contained sufficient line and shot. But regardless of his reasoning, the keeper's decision, combined with other oversights, proved fatal for him, his crew, and most of the sailors on the bark.

The events of that fateful night are not entirely certain, but at some point in the rescue attempt the surfboat overturned and Gale, three surfmen, and five Italian sailors drowned. The subsequent prevailing opinion held that the boat became swamped when the Italians in panic tried to board it "in a mob as soon as the surfboat came to the wreck." Three lifesavers and five sailors managed to climb back on the *Nuova Ottavia*, and although local residents sighted them and attempted to use the beach apparatus to save them, their unfamiliarity with the equipment resulted in failure. The locals exhausted all the shot in their futile effort to reach the wreck with a line. In the afternoon of March 2 the bark broke up, and the remaining surfmen and a sailor drowned. Only four Italians survived, making their way ashore on a piece of wreckage. A good many more men might have lived that day had the lifesavers not forgotten to wear the cork life jackets that the service provided them. Kimball had adopted the jackets for his surfmen shortly after assuming his duties as chief of the Revenue Marine.

No one could question the bravery of the seven lifesavers who lost their own lives trying to save the sailors aboard the *Nuova Ottavia*. In fact, in recognition of the North Carolinians' gallantry, the consul general of Italy, by order of that country's Department of Foreign Affairs and Marine and at the request of the Italian Society for Salvage, awarded $408 in gold to the families of the deceased Jones Hill surfmen, the first North Carolinians to die in the service. But even though the failed rescue proved the heroism of the state's lifesavers, it also demonstrated how far they had to go to become an effective organization.

In the first place, the rescue probably could have been made using the beach apparatus, thereby eliminating the possibility of a capsized surfboat. The keeper and his men also apparently failed to maintain discipline and keep order among the Italian sailors, thus allowing the excited and frightened crew to overturn the lifeboat in their haste to clamor aboard en masse. Finally, the lifesavers committed the cardinal mistake of neglecting to don their life jackets, a violation of one of the most fundamental rules of maritime safety.

Obviously, the United States Lifesavers of North Carolina had much to learn and improve before they would become an efficient and professional team. And the worst was not over. Other events soon unfolded that almost ended the career of the North Carolina service when it had scarcely begun.

Chapter 3
Huron and Metropolis

The United States warship *Huron* was unique in several ways. She was one of eight new warships, authorized by Congress in 1873, the construction of which marked an end to the nation's "old navy" built of wood and iron. Five of the mandated vessels were wooden gunboats, and three—*Alert, Ranger,* and *Huron*—became the last iron warships ever constructed by the United States Navy, which in 1882 began building its ships of steel. The *Huron* also could claim the distinction of being one of the last United States warships to use both sail and steam power and smoothbore guns.

Workmen laid the keel of the *Huron* at the Delaware River Shipbuilding Company in Chester, Pennsylvania, in 1873. She was completed and commissioned on November 15, 1875. The navy designated her and her sister ships as third-rate gunboats, meaning that they carried a third less armament than a first-rate ship. As a sloop of war, the 541-ton *Huron* had iron plating and schooner-rigged sails (although her sail arrangement was scheduled to be changed to a barkentine rig like that of the *Alert* and *Ranger*). A two-cylinder, back-acting compound engine supplied her steam power. The *Huron's* ordnance included five large smoothbore guns, a Gatling gun, and an assortment of small arms. She also carried a number of small boats: two launches, a cutter, a whaleboat, a dinghy, a gig, and two life rafts called balsas.

After commissioning, the *Huron* served two years with the North Atlantic Squadron, as well as in Mexican waters and surveying the northern coast of South America and the islands of the Lesser Antilles. Commander Charles C. Carpenter served as her first captain, and Commander George P. Ryan succeeded him in September 1876. In November 1877 the ship departed New York, where she had been overhauled, bound for Havana, Cuba, with orders "to make a reconnaissance of the coast of Cuba, determining the doubtful points in positions, in coastline and in outlying dangers."

The *Huron* stopped en route at Hampton Roads, Virginia, on November 17 to complete outfitting. While in port, Commander Ryan received word from the secretary of the navy to await the arrival of a draftsman from Washington, D.C., who would assist in the survey of the Cuban coast. The draftsman, John J. Evans, arrived, and the *Huron* got under way on November 23 with 132 men on board. In setting his course southward, Commander Ryan chose to sail close to the North Carolina shoreline to avoid traveling against the Gulf Stream or taking the time-consuming and longer alternative of going out beyond the stream. As in so many cases off the coast of the Old North State, that decision proved fatal.

Like an ominous precursor of disastrous events, a storm with gale-force winds struck in late afternoon and tore away the *Huron*'s staysail, forcing the crew to set a storm sail and reef up most of the other sails. After passing Currituck Lighthouse and before reaching Bodie Island light, the officers on duty—hindered by darkness, rough seas, and dense fog—failed to vary their course accurately according to the configuration of the North Carolina coastline. As a result, the *Huron* ran too close to the shore and suddenly, without warning, struck hard aground near Nags Head.

United States warship *Huron*. Engraving from *Harper's Weekly* (1877).

George P. Ryan, *Huron* commander. Engraving from *Harper's Weekly* (1877).

At first the officers thought that they had struck a shoal-covered wreck eight to ten miles out to sea. None realized how close to the beach their vessel really was until it was too late. When he finally saw the North Carolina coastline through the fog, Commander Ryan cried, "My God! How did we get in here?!"

In the midst of howling winds and crushing waves breaking over the steamer's decks, an attempt to back her off the shoal failed. Water poured into the engine room as collapsing spars and rigging fell through the hatch covers. The crew rushed to put the cutter overboard, but damage to its hull quickly sank it. Some of the sailors tried without much success to cut away the sails and masts and throw the guns into the water to lighten the ship in the hope that she would drift off the shoal that imprisoned her. The shooting of flares to summon help from the beach produced no response as the violent waves continued to beat upon the vessel unmercifully. The *Huron* ultimately turned at an angle on her port side, and the majority of the crew "gathered together on the upper side of the forecastle, suffering much from the cold and exposure." Others hung or lashed themselves to rigging and the bowsprit. Commander Ryan and a subordinate officer perished when they unsuccessfully attempted to launch another lifeboat. The tremendous swells churning across the deck continued to tear away the grips of the clutching sailors and hurl them to their deaths.

The hopes of the wretched crew rose when just before dawn on November 24 they sighted a moving light on shore. They shouted with all that was in them both in jubilation and in an effort to summon their anticipated rescuers. Their hopes were soon dashed, however, for the light belonged merely to some fishermen who had earlier spotted the flares fired from the *Huron* and walked to the beach to investigate. But without lifesaving equipment the people ashore had no means to launch a rescue and could only stand by and watch the horrible scene unfold.

The ultimate and tragic irony was that the Nags Head Lifesaving Station stood only two-and-one-half miles south of the disaster. But in keeping with the Lifesaving Service's then current operating procedure, it remained closed and locked until the next month, when the active season began. The keeper apparently was at his home on Roanoke Island. The local inhabitants had no authority to break into the station to obtain the beach apparatus and had no training in its operation, even if they had tried to use it.

Sunrise found the *Huron* survivors still huddled in the forecastle or clinging to halyards, spars, rigging, or the bowsprit. But as they grew more fatigued and the cruel sea fiercer in its attack on the wreck, more of them lost their lives to the unrelenting bombardment of wind and water. Almost every wave breaking over the vessel washed someone overboard, tumbling the helpless victims head over heels like rag dolls before finally drowning them.

Growing higher and higher, the seas carried executive officer S. A. Simmons over the side twice, and both times he clamored back aboard. Then, as if in angry retaliation for his tenacity, a third surge tossed him from his perch and drowned him. Sweeping over the entire ship, one large wave snatched away and drowned twelve men at once.

The seas around the wreck continued to climb, swelling from six to eight feet in depth. Realizing that the ship soon would be entirely swamped and that no help was likely from shore, Ensign Lucien Young called for volunteers to help him launch the one balsa remaining on the littered deck. Amid the wreckage, he and Seaman Antonio Williams eventually wrestled the balsa over the side and crawled down into it. After they cut the three-inch line by which they lowered the raft, they became entangled in the collapsed rigging and were struck several times by the spars as they washed up against the ship. The balsa then drifted toward the stern of the *Huron*, where a heavy surf capsized it. Damaged spars and other wreckage pinned both men underwater and nearly drowned them, but they somehow freed themselves and grasped the raft. They remained in the water and tried to swim and simultaneously steer the balsa to avoid its turning over again, but another large swell tossed them a second time. Ensign Young captured the raft and pushed it toward Williams, who had been thrown about ten feet by the wave. Williams pulled himself into the raft and stood up, looking desperately for a point of reference. The seaman sighted a number of telegraph poles on shore, which he mistook for the masts of fishing boats, and the two men began to steer toward them. They capsized twice more but finally and miraculously hit the beach about three-quarters of a mile north of the *Huron*. Near the site where they landed, Young and Williams discovered two other seamen, alive and lying in the surf, too exhausted to move further. They pulled them on shore, rested briefly, and then hurried down the beach in search of assistance to rescue the sailors remaining on the wreck.

Meanwhile, aboard the *Huron* other members of the crew, realizing that any chance for rescue from shore was fast slipping away, attempted to swim to safety. Cadet Engineer W. T. Warburton lowered himself into the water, where the current immediately seized him. Drifting north, he managed to stay afloat and eventually washed aground about a mile north of the disaster. There a strong undertow caught him and nearly dragged him back out to sea. Luckily two local residents pulled him from the water. Some other sailors, swept from the vessel as seas continued to wash men overboard, reached shore safely. Among the fortunate few to make it alive was Master William P. Conway. Williams and Young encountered him emerging from the surf as they hurried along the beach toward the group of locals gathered to view the wreck. The ensign asked the bystanders to patrol along the shoreline to look for victims who might make the beach and assist them if possible. He also dispatched a rider on horseback to the telegraph station at Kitty Hawk to send a message to Washington for help from the navy. It was then about seven o'clock in the morning.

Young asked the Bankers why they had not used the lifesaving equipment at the station to aid the *Huron* crew. They responded that they found the station locked and were afraid to break into it without official permission. Young then persuaded five volunteers to go with him to the station. They broke into the building and dragged out the beach apparatus equipment, which they placed in the horse-drawn cart of Dare County sheriff Brinkley, who had just arrived at the site. Back on the wreck the mainmast fell across the smokestack and into the water. Then two other crewmen, Master W. S. French and Captain of Guard Michael Trainor, attempted to swim to safety. Trainor reached the beach, where two men pulled him from the water. French, however, disappeared, and his body was never recovered.

Ensign Young, Sheriff Brinkley, and the volunteers did not arrive at the scene of the wreck until about eleven o'clock. As they drew near, they saw the mizzenmast fall. No one alive remained aboard the vessel, which was almost completely sub-merged. Sometime in perhaps late morning or early afternoon Nags Head keeper B. F. Meekins, who had been summoned from Roanoke Island, arrived at the site. "On Saturday morning, No-vember 24, 1877," Meekins later reported, "I was informed that a man-of-war was wrecked on the coast about three miles above my station. I hastened to the wreck and summoned T. T. Toler, J. T. Wescott, W. W. Dough, James Howard, Willis Tillett and Bannis-ter Gray for my crew and was soon ready for action." Whatever time Meekins and his men finally arrived, there remained nothing to be done but to search for victims in the surf and care for the survivors. Meekins subsequently recorded in his log that his life-savers helped to resuscitate three sailors from near death. For a while, the exhausted and battered survivors lay exposed on the beach. The bodies of the recovered dead were laid in a row. Persons on the beach began helping the still-living victims to a nearby fishing shack, where a fire and blankets warmed them. Cadet Engineer Warburton later recalled: "I was taken to a shanty, where I found a fire lighted and a dry blanket. . . . I had no idea how long I was in the water. I was so bruised that I couldn't move when I got ashore and was obliged to remain in the shanty 'til later in the afternoon. When Mr. Conway decided to move the party to the lifesaving station, I was carried in Sheriff Brinkley's cart."

As Sheriff Brinkley transported the men to Nags Head Station, they were provided with food, clothing, and bedding. The surfmen and volunteers continued to search for more survivors and bodies. Their efforts ultimately revealed that of the 132 men who had left Hampton Roads aboard the *Huron* on November 23 only 34 remained alive. The four officers—Young, Conway, War-burton, and Assistant Engineer R. G. Denig—spent the night of the twenty-fourth at Brinkley's house, and the thirty crewmen stayed at the lifesaving station.

In the meantime the distress message sent by the United States Signal Service operator at Kitty Hawk to Norfolk and

Washington had excited a response from the Navy Department, which telegraphed Baker Brothers, a Norfolk wrecking company, to dispatch their wrecking steamer *B & J Baker* to Nags Head. The navy also ordered three of its steamers—*Swatara*, *Powhatan*, and *Fortune*—to the scene.

The ships arrived off Nags Head early on the morning of the twenty-fifth. Aboard the *B & J Baker* was John J. Guthrie, superintendent of District No. 6, who had hastily departed his headquarters at Portsmouth, Virginia, and joined the vessel at Old Point Comfort. The wrecking ship's passengers also included Henry L. Brooke, a reporter for the *Norfolk Virginian*. The steamers remained offshore for a considerable time because the rough waves and surf made a landing with a boat too hazardous. But at three o'clock in the afternoon Captain E. M. Stoddard, commanding the *B & J Baker*, ordered a boat lowered over the side. The launch carried Stoddard, Guthrie, Brooke, six seamen as oarsmen, and Stoddard's dog. Once under way, the boat made toward the beach in "good style" until it reached a point about one hundred yards south of the *Huron* and two hundred yards from the shore. There it surmounted a huge wave and "shot ahead." A second large breaker, however, arose behind and overtook the launch and "in a twinkling hoisted the surfboat broadside on, and catching it on the crest of the waves, threw it bottom upwards about ten feet in the air."

Stoddard, Brooke, and a seaman managed to catch hold of the capsized boat and held on until dragged through the surf to the beach. Another of the oarsmen managed to swim to shore and the frightened dog swam back to the *B & J Baker*. But Guthrie and four seamen drowned, thus bringing the death toll of the *Huron* incident to 103.

Fortunately for the *Huron* survivors, a naval relief party with supplies and medical assistance had arrived about one o'clock, via the inland canal from Norfolk. Even earlier the small steamer *Bonita* had tied up on the sound side of Nags Head, and its captain offered to take the victims to Norfolk. Late in the afternoon the battered and bedraggled survivors—some walking, others riding in carts—crossed over from the ocean side to a wharf on the sound, boarded the *Bonita*, and departed for Norfolk, leaving behind the corpses of many of their comrades.

For a number of days after the wreck of the *Huron*, bodies continued to wash ashore along the North Carolina and Virginia coasts, some more than thirty miles away. Search parties temporarily buried some of the deceased. Keeper B. F. Meekins of Nags Head Station noted that "the bodies who were thrown on shore by the waves were taken the best care of possible. There were two bodies lashed to the wreck. These I took off and buried."

On November 27 Lieutenant Commander J. G. Greene and a naval detachment arrived at Nags Head and began retrieving and preparing for shipment to permanent burial sites the corpses of the drowned *Huron* crew. Their task lasted two weeks. Deterioration and the loss of personal effects by the victims made their job difficult. Only tattoos identified some of the sailors whose features had badly decomposed.

A public outcry followed the *Huron* catastrophe. Many of the leading East Coast newspapers recounted the grisly details of the incident and began attacking the Lifesaving Service for a lack of professionalism and diligence in North Carolina. "The disaster might have been greatly lessened had our lifesaving station been what it should have been," declared a Boston editorialist. "This branch of our service has proved to be sadly weak and undisciplined, and more organization is needed all along the coast." How was it, some newspapers asked, that such a tremendous loss of life occurred only a short distance from a lifesaving station? "The ship struck within two hundred yards of the shore, and two miles of a life-saving station that was one in name and name only," the *Norfolk Virginian* angrily noted. That the stations were not even opened for the year and would not be opened for another week when the *Huron* went down especially engendered alarm and concern among members of the press and their readers. Editors immediately began calling for a longer active season. The Elizabeth City *Economist* complained: "The ill-fated *Huron* teaches us that the 1st of December is too late for the commencement of the duties of the Lifesaving Service. In the name of humanity . . . let the service begin on the first day of November." The *Norfolk Landmark* went even further and proclaimed: "The crews should be on duty all year, had the station been manned . . . all of the [*Huron's*] officers and men would in all probability be living today." The *Virginian* sarcastically observed that

unfortunately for them the government of their country had decided that no shipwreck occurring before the first of December should be expected or provided for. What superior intelligence it was that ordained and regulated the system of life-stations we know not, nor can we understand the executive wisdom that fixed that date as the time from which they should be manned and prepared to carry out the objects of their institution. The experiences of mariners on this coast, it seems would suggest that the months of September, October and November are especially fruitful of storms. The life-saving system, however, seems to proceed upon the supposition that water will not drown men unless the temperature is at the freezing point. The fate of the Huron is a terrible refutation of this idea. We trust it will provide a warning that shall not be disregarded. Had the station in the vicinity of which the Huron struck been properly manned and in efficient working order, there is little doubt that many, perhaps all, of the lost might have been saved from the wreck. As it was, for hours the poor fellows battled for life against the sea, in sight of a government institution ordained for the purpose of their rescue, while no rescue came, because forsooth their misfortune was one week of the time fixed by the government for the succor of shipwrecked mariners. If our vessels and our merchants are expected to navigate our coast the year round, why in the name of common sense are the means intended for their assistance limited to one-half the year? The lesson taught is a grievous one. It convicts some one, whether Congress or the Executive Department, of a grievous blunder, one that has brought sorrow and desolation to a hundred homes.

In response to such outcries, the Lifesaving Service could only plead a lack of funding to establish a sufficient number of stations, opened for adequate periods, and to pay for qualified keepers and surfmen and proper equipment and training. Even *Harper's Weekly* expressed dismay at the seeming lack of preparedness displayed by the service. In a December 1877 issue of the magazine, a satirical Thomas Nast cartoon portrayed an exasperated Uncle Sam standing at Nags Head looking over the *Huron* wreck and musing: "I suppose I must spend a little on Lifesaving. . . ."

As if to ensure and reinforce Uncle Sam's resolve, tragedy struck again on the Tar Heel coast almost before the victims of the *Huron* disaster could be finally laid to rest. The new tragedy involved the steamer *Metropolis*, and before it was over another eighty-five people had lost their lives in the deadly waters off the North Carolina coast.

The steamship *Metropolis* had a suspicious past. Although rigged and equipped for the merchant trade by 1878, she had been the Federal gunboat *Stars and Stripes* during the Civil War. The ship had served on the North Carolina coast and participated in the Battle of Roanoke Island in 1862 and in subsequent operations on the state's sounds. After the war the owners changed the vessel's name, refitted her, and fraudulently altered her papers to take years off her age.

In January 1878 the Philadelphia contractors P. and T. Collins Company chartered the vessel out of New York. The Collins firm recently had won a contract with the Bolivian Navigation Company to build a railroad in Brazil to circumvent the falls and rapids at the junction of the River Madeira and the Mamore River. The new railroad would greatly improve Bolivia's trade and transportation route down the Madeira and Amazon rivers to the Atlantic coast. P. and T. Collins hired the *Metropolis* to transport workmen (mostly Irish) and cargo from Philadelphia to Brazil. The company already had dispatched another ship, the *Mercedita*, filled

Thomas Nast cartoon of Uncle Sam musing over *Huron* wreck at Nags Head. From *Harper's Weekly* (1877).

with men and equipment. Unbeknown to the Philadelphia con-tractor, however, another charter for the *Metropolis* had been canceled a month earlier by the Atlantic Coastline Railroad when the steamer, hired to convey freight from Norfolk to Wilmington, had become disabled and was towed into the Virginia port by a navy ship. Later, rumors and allegations circulated that the *Me-tropolis* was unseaworthy—even rotten in some places—and that her engines were too small for her size.

Near the end of January the *Metropolis*, outfitted with additional lifeboats, arrived at Philadelphia from New York and began taking on cargo and passengers. On the twenty-eighth, amid many tender and tearful farewells by their families who crowded the Reading Railroad dock, 215 laborers boarded the ship bound for Brazil. Also aboard when she pulled away from the wharf carrying one thousand tons of iron rails, stores, and coal were thirteen crewmen and twenty saloon passengers, including three women. On the following day the *Metropolis* reached the open sea and began the voyage to South America—a destination she would never reach.

Trouble soon struck when the vessel encountered rough weather. The passengers became seasick, and the iron rails in the hold began to shift about dangerously. A cry that fire had broken out incited panic until it proved to be a false alarm. More real was the discovery that a leak had occurred aft near the rudderpost, rising waist deep and causing the engines to strain under the added weight. Just about the time that the ship passed Chesapeake Bay, Captain J. H. Ankers ordered the cargo of coal thrown over the side so that the pumps could expel the water then pouring into the hold. The passengers formed a bucket brigade to throw the coal overboard, and as a result of their efforts the pumps made headway. But those bailing hardly had time to set down their buckets before more water poured in from widening seams rent in the hull by the shifting of the iron rails with the violent movement of the ship.

The overworked pumps broke down, and the bucket brigade formed again.

While the *Metropolis* strained southward, the storm worsened, and so did circumstances aboard the vessel. The engines labored as the water level continued to climb in the hold. Then suddenly, as the ship neared Currituck Beach, a tremendous wave crashed over the deck, tearing away the smokestack, seven of the lifeboats, the after mainsail, and other portions of the vessel. Almost simultaneously water in the engine room drowned the engine fires. Virtually disabled, the *Metropolis* floundered helplessly. Seeing the Currituck Beach Lighthouse and realizing that his vessel could not survive much longer, Captain Ankers ordered the remaining sails set and began sailing for the shore.

Just before dawn on the thirty-first the ship struck an outer bar, washed over it—losing in the process several passengers who tumbled overboard and drowned—and finally lodged on an inner bar about one hundred yards from the beach. Those on board first thought they had reached safety and gave out a cheer. But their jubilation soon ended when they discovered that a strip of angry sea with huge breakers still raged between them and the beach and that they were a long way from being out of danger. Some of them struggled into life jackets. Six men succeeded in launching a lifeboat, and three more jumped over the side of the *Metropolis* and began swimming. All of those nine made it safely to shore and set out along the beach in search of help to rescue those who remained on board the stricken steamer. They eventually staggered to a local hunting club, where they received dry clothes and club owner John J. Dunton dispatched a messenger with news of the tragedy to the Jones Hill Lifesaving Station, over four miles north of the wreck site. But at the station Keeper John G. Chappell had already received word of the disaster from Swepson C. Brock, a local resident who had ridden a horse to the outpost with news of the *Metropolis*. Chappell mounted behind Brock, and the two men started on horseback for the wreck. The keeper instructed his surfmen to follow as quickly as possible with the handcart containing the beach apparatus. En route to the scene of the catastrophe, Chappell and Brock passed wreckage and bodies from the *Metropolis* that had washed ashore.

Meanwhile, the six lifesavers from Jones Hill Station— William Perry, Jim Rogers, John Rogers, Sam Gillett, Nat Gray, and Piggott Gilliken—had virtually exhausted themselves attempting to pull and push the heavy handcart containing the beach apparatus through the deep sand. They had traveled only a mile and a half when John Dunton and the survivors who had staggered to the hunting club overtook them on their way back to the *Metropolis* scene. Dunton was riding a pony, which he hitched to the cart, and with the aid of the animal in pulling the apparatus, the lifesavers finally reached the wreck site about 12:30 P.M. They saw many of the *Metropolis* passengers still clinging to the ship and immediately followed Chappell's orders to set up the beach apparatus.

But the subsequent rescue attempt was plagued by a series of mistakes and bad luck. When the keeper fired off the shot line the attached ball from the mortar flew over but well beyond the wreck, and before anyone on board could secure the line it fell into the water. The surfmen drew the line back to shore and coiled it again. Chappell aimed the mortar lower on the second try and managed to land the shot line on a yardarm. The second mate crawled along the yardarm and grasped the line, but when he passed it down to his shipmates it still hung precariously over the spar. And as the men aboard the wreck began pulling the heavy tail block and whip to the vessel with the shot line, the latter scraped and wore against the yardarm and eventually broke. The tail block fell back into the sea.

The surfmen hauled in the shot line again and spliced on a new section. Keeper Chappell prepared to fire another round, but his heart sank when he discovered that he had no more gunpowder to charge the mortar. In an incredible oversight, only enough powder had been placed in the cart to fire two shots. More than enough powder existed back at the station, but that was over four miles away, and both horses had been dispatched on separate missions. One rider had departed to alert the telegraph operator at Kitty Hawk to send word of the *Metropolis* to headquarters, and the other had gone to summon more lifesavers. Swepson Brock, however, had enough gunpowder at his nearby residence for a number of shots, and with that the keeper loaded the mortar again. But the macabre comedy of errors continued when the next two attempts separated the shot from the shot line. As the last mortar round broke from the line (which had been tied to the shot with proper knots but may have been rotten) and splashed into the sea beyond the *Metropolis*, it ended any possibility of using the beach apparatus to save those remaining aboard the wreck.

Seeing what had happened on the beach, the victims realized that they would have to reach safety by their own means, as their ship was almost falling apart beneath their feet. The mainmast tumbled to the deck and what remained of the cabin swept overboard with several passengers still clutching it. A hell-like pandemonium reigned as the survivors frantically tried to find life buoys, were caught or struck unconscious by fallen rigging, or washed away, in some cases to be hit by rolling debris and killed. Keeper Chappell donned a rubberized, watertight suit and attempted to swim a line to the disintegrating vessel. But he failed and had to be dragged back ashore by his lifesavers.

Meanwhile swimmers and bodies began washing onto the beach with every surge of the surf. An unconscious Captain Ankers, also dressed in a rubberized suit, improperly fitted and full of water, was pulled from the sea and resuscitated by the surfmen. For over a mile along the shore, lifesavers, volunteers, and recovered victims ventured into the dangerous surf to rescue survivors. The last of them reached shore as night fell and large fires of driftwood were lighted. Dr. G. D. Green, the ship's surgeon, who had managed to reach safety, tried to attend to the injured, who

Aftermath of *Metropolis* wreck. Engraving from *Frank Leslie's Illustrated Newspaper* (1878); copy by North Carolina Collection.

were transported by horse cart or on men's backs to nearby houses, the hunting club, or the Currituck Beach Lighthouse. Others—cold, exhausted, and hungry—spent the night huddled by the fires. In the morning relief parties began arriving on the scene.

In the interim the telegram from the Signal Service outpost at Kitty Hawk had reached Washington, D.C., and the chief of the Signal Service had ordered the local operator to

Collecting bodies from *Metropolis* disaster. Engraving from *Frank Leslie's Illustrated Newspaper* (1878); copy by North Carolina Collection.

Currituck Beach to open a telegraph line there. From Norfolk the navy had dispatched four relief vessels, and two wrecking companies had sent one ship each. Having been fed and clothed and had their injuries attended to, the survivors ultimately reached Norfolk on Saturday, February 2, on board the steamer *Cygnet*. At 9:07 the next morning the Signal Service telegraph operator at Currituck Beach sent the following message to his chief in Washington:

Have gained all information possible this morning and during the night. The Life-saving Service patrolled the beach all night. Six dead bodies were found, five of which were found 11 miles north of the wreck. They were buried by the life-saving crew, and spot marked where buried. There was nothing on the bodies to identify them. The excitement has died away. All have left the wreck. Property sold at auction and everything is quiet. Station No. 4 buried a man washed up a little distance south of station at 4:30 P.M. He was naked, having gray hair and mustache, aged about 50 years.

The final six bodies reported by the telegraph operator brought the total deaths from the *Metropolis* to eighty-five. At Norfolk the survivors received further care and began leaving for their various destinations on February 5.

Just as with the wreck of the *Huron* less than two weeks earlier, the *Metropolis* disaster produced a tremendous public outcry against the Lifesaving Service and the North Carolinians living on the Outer Banks. "It begins to be painfully clear," declared the New York *World* on February 3, "that the terrible loss of Human life which attended the shipwreck of the Metropolis on the North Carolina coast Thursday must be attributed directly to the inefficiency of the Life-Saving Service."

The *New York Times* joined the attack and stated that the *Huron* and *Metropolis* disasters had made it obvious that the Lifesaving Service sorely needed reform and improvement. "That the Life-saving service can and should be vastly improved is patent to all in the light of the recent disasters," declared the editorialist "Civil Service" on February 4. He continued:

Superintendents must be appointed for life, or during good behavior, if personal and political pressure is not to have a great deal to do with appointment to minor positions. It is useless for Chief Kimball to protest politics have nothing to do with the service. They do, and always will, so long as the present method is maintained. There is now, upon the New Jersey coast, a station Captain, who never was at sea, does not know how to feather an oar, or even swim, who was retained by the Superintendent to the exclusion of more skillful [men] simply because of his political activity. Secondly, the crews should be drilled and subjected to systematic discipline, as they are in other countries; uniformed in an inexpensive manner; inspected frequently by their superintendents, and an esprit de corps established, as it is possible to do in any service properly managed, with an inspecting officer with his heart in his work.

Now, for the most part, the men take their stool ducks [sic] and oyster-rakes to the beach, live in the station-house, and all the rowing or practicing they do is to paddle ashore to sell the products of shot-gun or oyster rakes. On some stations there are crews who could not row together in unison for their lives. In short, they look upon it as an easy way of getting $40 a month when there is nothing doing in the Winter.

Lastly and most important is the necessity of a law admitting to the pension list the wives and children of all such as lose their lives while in the discharge of their duties. They are twenty fold more dangerous than those of the average man-of-war sailor. As one [lifesaver] expressed it to the writer: "I wasn't afeered of anything until I came under petticoat gov'ment. But with a wife an' four young uns hanging on a man to keep 'em from the poor-house, he gits to be womanish hisself." Knowing wife and children would be taken care of, the men would be much braver and readier to take risks.

The *Boston Evening Transcript* attributed the Lifesaving Service's failure to save more lives from the *Huron* and *Metropolis* to the "great difficulty . . . experienced in getting competent keepers for the stations along the North Carolina coast."

The northern press also vented its anger at the residents of the Outer Banks, who, it claimed, robbed the bodies of the victims from the *Metropolis*. Such accusations derived primarily from the testimony of William H. Harrison, the man in charge of the Brazil-bound laborers on the *Metropolis*, who lost his wife in the wreck. After Harrison returned to Philadelphia, the P. and T. Collins Company dispatched him back to North Carolina to have the bodies of the victims "taken up for the purpose of identification." Harrison brought coffins with him in which to place the bodies for shipment home. On February 10 he telegraphed that "to this (Sunday) morning I have taken up fifty bodies. They without exception have been robbed of all the things whereby I could possibly identify them. I am satisfied the robbing was done in many cases by some survivor, and in the [other] cases by the lower class of whites and negroes from the main land, who seemed to think that they had the right to take anything and everything they could lay hands to. The fact is, they not only robbed the dead by night, but also in open daylight."

A few unscrupulous North Carolinians may have robbed the corpses from the *Metropolis*, but Harrison's testimony was at best suspect, for he himself was arrested in Norfolk on a charge of robbing the bodies of the victims. Detectives discovered in his possession several trunks and "considerable clothing, bearing the marks of Civil Engineer Moore and others of the wrecked passengers." Thus Harrison may have accused North Carolinians of robbery merely to cover his own thievery. In any event, there was no evidence to support the claims of some northern newspapers that the people of Hatteras Island "plundered" the bodies of the drowned passengers and crew of the *Metropolis*. Captain James H. Merryman of the Revenue Marine, an inspector of the Lifesaving Service, exonerated the North Carolinians in the vicinity of the *Metropolis* wreck of charges of misconduct and commended them for their assistance during the disaster. He reported that a number of the Bankers cared for survivors in their homes "and fed and clothed them to the full extent of their means" and that "their generous hospitality is worthy of all praise." Among the locals who came to the aid of the victims, John J. Dunton, S. C. Brock, Josephus Baum, T. J. Poyner, and lighthouse keeper N. G. Burris received special recognition by Merryman. Affidavits by some of the survivors also testified to the kind treatment given them by the people of Currituck Beach and vicinity. Even Harrison himself tried to blame the robbery on "mainland" folk and confessed that "I have found some of the best men on this beach that I ever met in my life . . . men who helped to save the lives of many . . . and, in fact, took clothing off their backs and gave it to the survivors."

The Tar Heel Lifesaving Service, however, still faced the clamorous charges of incompetency and political favoritism. As a result, the United States Senate passed a resolution on February 6, 1878, seeking from John Sherman, secretary of the treasury, "information in relation to the present condition and state of efficiency of the life-saving service on the coast of North Carolina." In a letter sent to the Senate ten days later Sherman defended the skill and courage of the North Carolina surfmen. He stressed that operations on their coast were seriously hindered by the distance—about ten miles—existing between the too-few stations located there. The stations from Cape Cod to Delaware, on the other hand, stood only four to five miles apart. The secretary explained how the great gaps between the lifesaving outposts delayed the beach patrol's coming upon a wreck and returning to a station to summon the crew. Using the *Metropolis* incident as an example, he stressed the difficulty and time required to pull the heavy lifesaving equipment for miles through deep sand. In the case of the *Metropolis* the beach apparatus cart, weighing over a thousand pounds, "had to be hauled by six men for four and one-half miles, over a beach in whose sands the feet of the men were imbedded deeply at every step, and the tires of their mortar cart, although five inches broad, sank four or five inches." Only the arrival of a man with a horse enabled the surfmen to reach the wreck by midday. Sherman pointed out that during the twenty-four hours before the *Metropolis* crashed ashore the surfmen at Jones Hill Station had walked long, exhausting patrols and were already tired. "A further point, common to all such cases," he claimed, "is presented by this, namely, that these men, upon whose unwasted vigor much of the success of their service at the wreck depended . . . arrived at the scene of their toil, still further wearied by the severe march with their apparatus, to at once engage in still more exhausting exertions." Increasing the number of stations and thereby bringing them closer together, claimed Sherman, would shorten the length of beach each crew had to patrol and enable neighboring stations to aid each other. In concluding his report to the Senate, the secretary recommended that to avoid such disasters as the *Huron* and *Metropolis* in the future, the federal government should increase the number of North Carolina stations "so as to bring them within an average distance of four or five miles of each other"; build five additional stations between the southernmost station and Cape Fear; raise the annual salary of keepers to as much as five hundred dollars and give them powers of customs inspectors; increase the number of lifesaving crew members at each station to eight; and extend the active season to run from September 1 to May 1 "or a longer period, if deemed expedient."

But not everyone in Washington believed that bolstering the Lifesaving Service was the answer to improving rescue operations. Within weeks of the *Metropolis* disaster, Senator Aaron A. Sargent of California introduced a bill (filed on February 19) to transfer the Lifesaving Service from the Department of the Treasury to the Department of the Navy, where "proper military discipline" could be maintained. Under the proposed reorganization, the secretary of the navy would appoint naval officers to be superintendents of lifesaving activities and transfer the keepers and surfmen to the navy to serve wherever ordered. The idea met considerable opposition in North Carolina. "It strikes us that this change would be most unfortunate," protested the

Elizabeth City *Economist*. "Naval officers are well enough in their place, perhaps, but that place is not saving life in the raging surf billows. There is too much red tape about them for that service. Too much 'pomp and circumstance,' too much tinsel and glitter, too much official etiquette, too much stilted and stately routine discipline." Opponents of a navy takeover emphasized the importance of having superintendents and crews familiar with conditions in the areas in which they served. "Experience has demonstrated that those who live near the sea make the best and most reliable surfmen," asserted the *Economist*. "The superintendent should not only be a man entirely reliable but one whose life has familiarized him with all the dangers of the surf. . . . Does any one believe that a Naval officer with a surf crew of naval marines, would compare, in efficiency, in promptness, in knowledge of the work and capacity to perform it, with a crew of native surfmen, under the charge, for instance, of such a man as Isaac C. Meekins, of Roanoke Island[?]"

When news of the Sargent bill reached the House of Representatives, Congressman James W. Covert of New York arose in the chamber to denounce a navy takeover and deliver a stirring defense of the current lifesaving system of staffing stations with experienced local residents. Such men, he insisted,

are among the best men of the community. They are men of intelligence, owning their homes, supporting families—thrifty, forehanded, and enterprising. During the season when not thus employed [as lifesavers], they are engaged mainly in surf-fishing; and in this way they gain correct and intimate knowledge of every foot of ground upon which they work and every phase and feature of the surf in which they labor. They do not depend upon the pittance received from the government for their support; it comes to them simply as a small addition to their yearly income, earned at seasons when they cannot prosecute their usual work. These men would not consent to enlist in the Navy, subject at the call of the Government to leave their families at any juncture, for possibly a long absence from home. Their home interests are in many instances too large; their home ties too strong, to permit many of them as prudent men to do this. This class of people have in great measure made the life-saving service what it is. They have established local reputations for bravery and devotion upon the occasion of many a sad scene of shipwreck and disaster. They are known and marked men. Any act of cowardice, and temporary faltering when duty called, would render them objects of by-word and reproach in the communities in which they live.

On March 25 Washington C. Whitthorne, representative from Tennessee, introduced the Sargent bill in the House. But House supporters of the Lifesaving Service offered a substitute bill (H.R. 3988, based on an 1877 bill by Representative Samuel S. Cox of New York) that would prevent a navy takeover and strengthen and extend the existing lifesaving system. In the House on June 3, a heated debate ensued between proponents of bill 3988 and the backers of the Sargent legislation. Among those who spoke passionately for the existing Lifesaving Service were North Carolina congressmen Jesse J. Yeates and Curtis H. Brogden, a former governor of the state. Yeates exalted the honor, character, and devotion to duty of the North Carolina surfmen and regretted only that he could not challenge personally each detractor of the Lifesaving Service. Brogden declared that government existed to preserve life and therefore could not turn its back on the victims of shipwrecks. He further argued that all the other government agencies for the protection of maritime commerce and revenues—the Lighthouse Board, the Revenue Marine Service, the Coast Survey, the Steamboat Inspection Service—operated under the supervision of the Department of the Treasury. Consequently, the Lifesaving Service belonged there also. Brogden's speech ended the House session for the day at 10:05 P.M.

When the House continued its discussion of the lifesaving bills on the morning of June 4, Representative Whitthorne insisted that the Lifesaving Service functioned "under the influence and control of politicians and local influence," and he reiterated the need for navy "discipline and organization" to perform lifesaving operations efficiently. But in a long speech Representative Cox refuted such charges and urged his congressional col-

North Carolina congressmen Jesse J. Yeates (*left*) and Curtis H. Brogden (former governor) defended the record of Tar Heel lifesavers. Engraving of Yeates from *The National Cyclopedia of American Biography*; photograph of Brogden from State Archives.

Thomas Nast cartoon proclaiming the Forty-fifth Congress's lifesaving bill "the only thing worth saving." From *Harper's Weekly* (1878).

leagues to forget political bias and save lives by passing bill 3988. After Cox spoke and the legislation was read for a third time, the House voted and passed the lifesaving bill, which then awaited its summons to the Senate. On June 17 New York senator Roscoe Conkling, the prominent Republican party leader and former candidate for the presidential nomination, introduced a motion to consider the House bill. After an attempt failed to amend it to require steamboats carrying passengers to have a certain number of "life-saving dresses," the Senate passed H.R. 3988.

Although party politics and patronage were a part of the motivation for the lifesaving legislation, apparently they did not play a large role in either support for or opposition to the new law. Both Democrats and Republicans voted for the final bill, and almost everyone in Congress seems to have agreed that something needed to be done about aiding ships in danger. The chief disagreement came over whether to keep the Lifesaving Service in the Department of the Treasury or to transfer it to the Department of the Navy. Representatives and senators from coastal states tended to favor the former course and may have done so, at least partly, with the possibility for patronage and funding for their states in mind. North Carolina congressman Yeates, for example, had a number of coastal counties in his constituency, and new federal appropriations there meant employment and income for his supporters. When news spread that the lifesaving bill had passed and that new stations and appropriations were on their way to the Tar Heel State, the Elizabeth City *Economist* trumpeted: "The appropriations for these great necessities of Eastern North Carolina were secured by the Hon. J. J. Yeates, our Representative in congress. While the work of building these is going on, let the people think of the benefits, and work to send Yeates back that he may 'do so again.'" The contention that coastal residents familiar with conditions in their regions made the most efficient and qualified keepers and surfmen was a valid and, for the most part, sincere argument for maintaining the current lifesaving system. But for the rest of its career as an agency drawing among local inhabitants for its personnel, the Lifesaving Service continued to suffer charges of political favoritism.

The act of June 18, 1878, authorized the construction of over thirty new stations throughout the country. Fifteen were designated for Virginia and North Carolina. The contracts for building the North Carolina outposts provided for "their

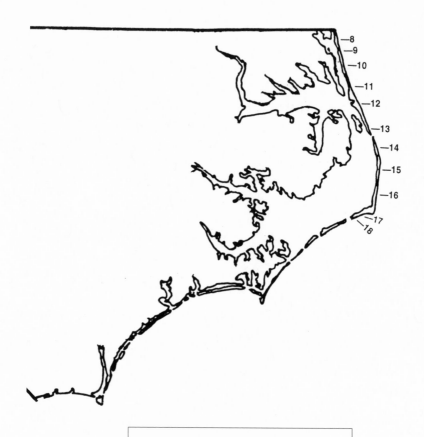

8. Deals Island (renamed Wash Woods)
9. Old Currituck Inlet (renamed Pennys Hill)
10. Poyners Hill
11. Paul Gamiels Hill
12. Kill Devil Hills
13. Tommys Hummock (renamed Bodie Island)
14. Pea Island
15. Cedar Hummock (renamed Gull Shoal)
16. Big Kinnakeet
17. Creeds Hill
18. Hatteras (renamed Durants)

NORTH CAROLINA STATIONS BUILT 1878

Kill Devil Hills Station. Photograph from collections of Library of Congress.

Big Kinnakeet Station. Photograph from North Carolina Collection.

Cedar Hummock (later called Gull Shoal) Station. Photograph from State Archives.

Sumner I. Kimball, national superintendent of Lifesaving Service. Engraving from *The National Cyclopedia of American Biography*.

completion by the 15th of November next, ready for occupancy which is as soon as they can be finished." By the winter of 1878-1879 eleven newly equipped and staffed stations stood ready for duty on the Tar Heel coast: Deals Island (later named Wash

Woods), Old Currituck Inlet (later called Currituck Inlet, then Pennys Hill), Poyners Hill, Paul Gamiels Hill, Kill Devil Hills, Tommys Hummock (north of Oregon Inlet and later named Bodie Island), Pea Island, Cedar Hummock (later called Gull Shoal), Big Kinnakeet, Creeds Hill, and Hatteras (later named Durants). All of the eleven new stations were located north of Hatteras Inlet.

The act of June 18 also removed the Lifesaving Service from the Revenue Marine Service and established it as a separate branch of the Department of the Treasury. The same legislation transferred Sumner I. Kimball, chief of the Revenue Marine, from that service and appointed him general superintendent of the Lifesaving Service. Kimball already had proven his considerable leadership capability when he had guided the service's operations when it was part of the Revenue Marine. Joseph W. Etheridge of Manteo received an appointment as the new district superintendent for District No. 6.

Although the new law made the Lifesaving Service an agency separate from the Revenue Marine, it still retained some connections with that parent organization. Captain James H. Merryman remained inspector of lifesaving stations, and along with Revenue Marine Captain John McGowan, he became co-superintendent for the construction of stations. Merryman appointed an assistant inspector for each district, and he assigned Lieutenant Walter Walton, also of the Revenue Marine, to that position in District No. 6. Inspectors at all levels made regular inspection tours. They noted the condition of equipment and frequency of training at each station, observed drills with beach apparatus and lifeboats, and verbally tested surfmen and keepers as to their duties. A medical officer frequently accompanied the inspection team to instruct the surfmen in resuscitation methods. Under the new organization, inspectors investigated every shipwreck that had a loss of life to determine the cause and, if any lifesaver had been derelict in his duty, to dismiss him from the service. The 1878 law also improved lifesaving operations by

David A. Lyle, inventor of Lyle gun. Photograph from *The National Cyclopedia of American Biography.*

increasing the length of the active season to eight months—September 1 to May 1. (Subsequently the active season was extended again, to August 1 through May 31 on the Atlantic and Gulf coasts.) To attract competent and experienced keepers, the legislation raised their salaries to four hundred dollars per year and gave them the powers of inspectors of customs.

In addition to legislation, certain technological developments made the Lifesaving Service more efficient. One of the most important of those changes was the adoption of the newly completed Lyle gun for use with the beach apparatus. In the autumn of 1878 Lieutenant David A. Lyle of the United States Army Ordnance Corps perfected a gun to supplant the mortars and other wreck artillery used throughout the service. Lighter and less bulky than its predecessors, the Lyle gun weighed 202 pounds when loaded with its eighteen-inch projectile. It could fire a maximum distance of 695 yards, thus adding significantly to the effective range of the shot line. The ease and reliability of loading the Lyle gun with a charge also made it an improvement over earlier guns. The reduction in weight of the new wreck ordnance and other parts

Pictured here with a twentieth-century coast guardsman, the Lyle gun remained in production until 1952. Photograph from State Archives.

Loading Lyle gun with charge. Photograph from State Archives.

of the beach apparatus made it easier for the surfmen to pull the beach cart (a major difficulty in the case of the *Metropolis*) to the site of a wreck. The task became even easier when the service soon began using horses or ponies to pull the carts and surfboats. Lyle's gun proved so vastly superior to the mortars and rockets that it replaced that it received almost worldwide acceptance and re-mained in production until 1952. Lyle continued his army career, simultaneously serving on the Treasury Department's Board on Lifesaving Appliances, until his retirement in 1909.

Thus, as the year 1878 came to a close, the Lifesaving Service received a new lease on life. Events in North Carolina—the wrecks of the *Huron* and *Metropolis*—had brought attacks of public outrage and indignation on the service, especially its Tar Heel component. The service had barely escaped being absorbed by the United States Navy. Subsequent performance would have to show whether the keepers and surfmen of North Carolina were worthy of the second chance bestowed on them.

Chapter 4
Brave Servants of Humanity

The Lifesaving Service began the new phase of its career in North Carolina amid still more controversy and even a sinister mystery. At 5:20 on the morning of November 30, 1879, Surfman Leonidas R. Tillett returned to the Pea Island Station from walking the south beat of the beach patrol. He made a fire in the galley stove, awakened the black female cook, and climbed the stairs to the second floor. Peering with binoculars from the south window, he spied a man whom he first believed to be a fisherman walking toward him along the beach. But looking more closely he discovered that the man wore no hat and that he might be shipwrecked. Tillett aroused Keeper George C. Daniels and the rest of the crew and bolted from the station to meet the staggering figure. Within a short distance he encountered the exhausted sailor—who could only mutter, "Captain drowned, masts gone"—and assisted him to the station.

Leaving the castaway in the care of the cook, Keeper Daniels and his surfmen started down the beach in search of a wreck. About a mile and a quarter south of their outpost they discovered debris in the surf and "at the same time, some part of the vessel rising and falling on the sea, about three hundred yards off shore." Then they followed the shoreline to New Inlet, about three-quarters of a mile further south, where they discovered more floating wreckage and began searching among it for bodies. At the inlet they met Ira, J. B., and W. A. Stowe, brothers and fishermen. The Stowes reported that they had found a survivor floating in the inlet and had carried him back to their camp on Jacks Shoal, an island in Pamlico Sound, and then returned to the beach to look for others. Daniels and two lifesavers crossed by boat to the shoal and left the remaining crew to search the beach. On the island the keeper discovered that the wrecked sailor had been resuscitated, given coffee, and wrapped in blankets by the Stowe brothers and "was so far recovered as to be out of danger." In crossing to the camp, however, Daniels had seen upon the beach "what appeared to be a man in a sitting position," and he sent the two surfmen back to investigate. With the aid of the Stowes, they returned with a third survivor, who was "insensible, and far gone, but breathing." The lifesavers treated him "as the first had been" and in the afternoon transported both men to the Pea Island Station. No other victims or bodies were found.

A subsequent investigation revealed that the three sur-vivors belonged to the seven-man crew of the three-masted schooner M & E Henderson. The 387-ton ship had been built at Pleasant Mills, New Jersey, in 1864 and was bound for Baltimore when she wrecked off the Carolina coast. Apparently she was thoroughly rotten and broke apart quickly after striking aground. First Lieutenant Charles F. Shoemaker, officer of the Revenue Marine and assistant inspector of the Lifesaving Service, described the wreck in his report of January 16, 1880:

Lying about two hundred and fifty yards off shore, was one of the vessel's spars, attached to some sunken portions of the wreck, near where she appears to have struck and went to pieces. Upon the shore opposite, lay parts of her plank-shear [sic], a section of her bow with breast-hooks attached, sections of her deck fast to parts of the beams, and broken masts, where they had been driven in the break up. From this point to New Inlet, three quarters of a mile farther south, the beach was strewn with fragments of the wreck. Occasional sound timbers, and a piece of new deck, were found, but the evidence of her rottenness, was too plain to be mistaken.

From 2 A.M. until daylight on the morning of the wreck the weather was clear, wind fresh N.E., a very heavy surf on the beach, and a strong southerly cut or current along shore.

The fact that the "Henderson", was laden with phosphate rock, that she struck the bar when a very heavy surf was running, that the main portions of the wreck landed on the beach almost opposite to where she appears to have struck, at any rate, to where all that was left of her in the water was found and still remains, added to the rottenness of the vessel, all give evidence of her sudden demolition[.] She could not have lasted more than one hour, and my judgment is that she did not hold together more than one half or three quarters of that time.

Besides her general unseaworthiness, other suspicious circumstances surrounded the M & E Henderson and her crash upon Tar Heel shores. One puzzling aspect of the disaster was the question of why only three deck hands out of a total crew of seven survived. Searchers found no trace of the others. Equally mystifying was the peculiar way in which the ship ran aground—in calm weather. Lieutenant Shoemaker concluded: "In view of the clear fine weather for some time before the vessel is supposed to have struck, which is testified to by all witnesses, one of two conclusions as to the cause of the disaster seems inevitable: either that the vessel was wrecked as the result of the gross carelessness and mismanagement of those in charge, or that she was purposely run ashore." That the survivors were foreigners, dark skinned, and spoke little English compounded the suspicions of federal authorities, who began to wonder if a mutiny had occurred aboard the M & E Henderson. After a term in jail the three sailors stood trial in Baltimore but went free for a lack of evidence, thus leaving the wreck of the M & E Henderson shrouded in mystery.

Keeper Daniels and some of his crew at Pea Island also came under investigation for their questionable performance of duty. Inspector Shoemaker reported that Surfman Tillett should and would have encountered the wreck on the night of the twenty-ninth if he had walked his patrol as prescribed. He recommended that Tillett "be discharged; cause, neglect of duty." The inspector also found that Daniels had deliberately falsified his report, claiming credit for rescue efforts he never performed. He called for the keeper's removal "immediately; cause, false swearing, and his personal acknowledgment of his unfitness for the position." Shoemaker further suggested that "surfman Charles L. Midgett be discharged; cause, not a competent surfman from lack of experience as admitted in his testimony." The Lifesaving Service accepted Shoemaker's report except that it retained Tillett at his post, although he soon left the station. The investigation and dismissals at Pea Island Station demonstrated that, despite recent reorganization and improvement, the Lifesaving Service was not competent throughout. But the actions taken in response to Shoemaker's report also set a precedent by emphatically making the point that in the future all stations would be strictly accountable and keepers and crews would have to toe the mark in performance.

Shoemaker set another precedent in the plan he proposed for reorganizing Pea Island Station (No. 17 in District 6). When accepted, his suggestion made North Carolina unique in the United States Lifesaving Service. He proposed that a black North Carolinian be appointed keeper at Pea Island. No African American had ever commanded a station in the entire country, and such an idea was audacious in 1879, especially in the South. To be sure, blacks had served as surfmen in North Carolina and elsewhere, but none had ever risen to keeper. "For appointment to the Keepership of Station No. 17," wrote the inspector, "I recommend Richard Etheridge, colored, now No. 6 surfman in Station No. 16 [Bodie Island, later named Oregon Inlet]. I examined this man, and found him to be thirty eight years of age, strong robust physique, intelligent, and able to keep the Journal of a station. He is reported one of the best surfmen on this part of the coast of North Carolina."

Shoemaker suggested that Etheridge's crew be composed of the two black surfmen already at Pea Island (William Davis and William Daniel), two from Caffeys Inlet Station (Lewis Wescott and Joseph Case), and two enlisted by Etheridge. The white men at Pea Island could be transferred to fill the vacancies at Caffeys Inlet and Etheridge's at Bodie Island Station, thus giving him an all-black staff. "I am aware," the inspector wrote to his superiors, "that no colored man holds the position of Keeper in the Lifesaving Service, and yet such as are surfmen, are found to be among the best on the coast of North Carolina. I have given this matter as careful consideration as I am capable of, and have tried to weigh every argument, for and against its adoption, and I am fully convinced that the efficiency of the service at this station, will be greatly enhanced by the adoption of my recommendations." Headquarters accepted Shoemaker's plan and gave Richard Etheridge command of Station No. 17. Black surfman Wescott declined to transfer to Pea Island, but William C. Bowser of Bodie Island Station took his place. To round out his crew, Etheridge hired George Midgett and Henry Daniel, two black watermen from Roanoke Island.

The keeper brought to his new position considerable experience and skill as both a lifesaver and a leader of men. Born in North Carolina in 1842, Etheridge was a free black living on Roanoke Island when the Federal army began recruiting former slaves in Union-held areas of the South to serve in its new black regiments. In September 1863 he enlisted in the Thirty-sixth Infantry Regiment, United States Colored Troops (originally called the Second Infantry Regiment, North Carolina Colored Volunteers). He quickly rose to the rank of sergeant, assisted in the recruitment of other blacks, and then served with his unit in the Virginia campaigns. As regimental commissary sergeant, he was

The United States's only all-black lifesaving crew: Keeper Richard Etheridge (*far left*) and surfmen of Pea Island Station. Photograph from State Archives.

discharged from the army at Brazos, Texas, in July 1866 and with his wife, Frances, returned to Roanoke Island, where he became a fisherman. Etheridge signed on with the Lifesaving Service at Bodie Island Station in 1877 and soon earned a reputation for courage and diligence.

As keeper at Pea Island Etheridge proved his mettle. In December 1881, for example, despite a high fever (possibly from malaria, which plagued North Carolina lifesavers) he led his surf-men, who went without food for an entire day, in the rescue of victims aboard the schooner *Thomas J. Lancaster*, bound from Boston to Savannah with a load of ice and wrecked at New Inlet in gale-force winds. The crew from the Chicamacomico Station (No. 18 in District 6) also participated in the rescue and provided the survivors with care and temporary quarters. A physician of the Revenue Marine Service at New Bern summoned aboard the cutter *Stevens* to attend the injured at Chicamacomico described the disaster:

> We learn that the loss of the schooner was a piece of gross carelessness on the part of the first mate, who had charge of her at the time she went ashore. There was no wind to speak of nor heavy sea at the time she struck, but in a short time a heavy storm arose, and there was no chance to get her off.
> There were on board the Captain and wife, three children, all girls, aged respectively 3, 5, and 11 years; eight of the crew. The lost were: the Captain and three children and first mate, cook and two sailors.
> Mrs. Hunter, the Captain's wife, was in the rigging twenty-four hours before being taken off, and the youngest child was found tied to the rigging by its feet, and head downwards. It is supposed the captain lost his life in trying to save the two oldest children after tying his wife and youngest child to the rigging, they having been washed overboard and he going for them, was lost with them.

The doctor further noted that had the crew remained on board and awaited the lifesavers more lives might have been saved. Three of them, however, jumped overboard and swam ashore. Four more followed and drowned. That left only the second mate to attach the shot line from shore, "which he was unable to do."

Not long before the wreck of the *Thomas J. Lancaster* the Pea Island Station had to be rebuilt. The first building had burned in May 1880. Lifesaving officials suspected arson, possibly resulting from racial hatred, and offered a reward for information leading to the apprehension of the incendiary. But no one was ever charged with the crime.

Toward the end of Richard Etheridge's career, he and his men "accomplished the near impossible," according to David Stick. When the schooner *E. S. Newman* wrecked near their outpost in October 1896, the raging wind and surging seas thwarted efforts to use standard equipment. But thinking fast, Etheridge improvised and called upon two of his strongest surfmen. He ordered a heavy line tied around the two. The other lifesavers held the other end of the line firmly while their two comrades bent into the wind and rose with the swelling breakers as they laboriously plodded to the stricken vessel. With another line, held in their hands, the rescuers lashed a sailor from the wreck to them and, thus carrying him, were pulled back to shore by their fellow surfmen. Using that method and taking turns wading two at a time to the *E. S. Newman*, the Pea Island men saved the lives of the nine persons on the ship, including the captain and a woman and child.

Etheridge's long and illustrious tenure as a United States lifesaver ended at his death in 1900. He died while on duty at the Pea Island Station, following several months of illness. He is buried near the site of his station, and his tombstone bears the inscription "We trust our loss will be his gain and with Christ he's gone to reign."

But the tradition of an African-American crew at Pea Island persisted after Richard Etheridge's death. That station remained the nation's only all-black facility even after the Lifesaving Service became part of the Coast Guard in 1915. At one point, in 1937, the Coast Guard replaced the black petty officer in charge at Pea Island with a white one. But a protest by black North Carolinians and Dare County white politician Robert Bruce Etheridge to Congressman Lindsay Warren led to the reinstatement of a black keeper. Thereafter African Americans manned the station until it closed in 1947.

During the 1880s Congress authorized the construction of six additional stations on the North Carolina coast, including for the first time several south of Hatteras Inlet. In 1881 there were 189 stations throughout the United States, with the largest number concentrated on the Atlantic coast. Others guarded the Gulf and Pacific coasts and the Great Lakes. One even stood sentinel at the dangerous falls of the Ohio River. Added to North Carolina's shores were the following stations: Cape Hatteras in 1880, New Inlet in 1882, Ocracoke (southwest of Hatteras Inlet and later named Hatteras Inlet Station) in 1883, Cape Fear (on Bald Head Island) in 1883, Oak Island in 1886, and Cape Lookout in 1888.

That decade also signaled notable innovations at stations throughout the country. In 1880 the Lifesaving Service purchased horses for its stations and thus authorized the official use of draft animals for pulling beach carts and surfboats to wreck sites. In some areas beach patrolmen also began riding horses on their beats. In that same year the Women's National Relief Association (later the Blue Anchor Society) started supplying clothing to the stations for the comfort of disaster survivors. In 1882 rates of pay for keepers and surfmen were raised, and the Board on Lifesaving Appliances was formally established to evaluate new and improved equipment for possible use by the service. In 1883 each North Carolina station began utilizing a seventh surfman in the winter months. The practice of establishing telephone connections between stations spread to the other districts after their successful employment in New Jersey in 1884. "These lines," reported a federal commission on economy and efficiency, "make it easy to concentrate the crews of two or more stations at any point where additional force is required."

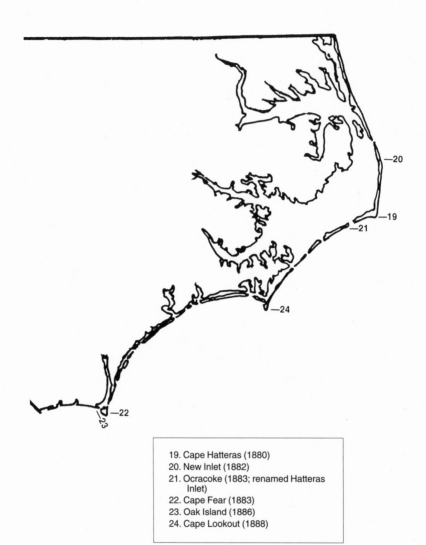

19. Cape Hatteras (1880)
20. New Inlet (1882)
21. Ocracoke (1883; renamed Hatteras Inlet)
22. Cape Fear (1883)
23. Oak Island (1886)
24. Cape Lookout (1888)

NORTH CAROLINA STATIONS BUILT 1880-1888

Cape Hatteras Station. Photograph from North Carolina Collection.

Cape Lookout Station. Photograph from State Archives.

Oak Island Station. Photograph from State Archives.

During the next decade the federal government built stations at Portsmouth in 1894 and Core Banks (later called Atlantic Station) in 1896. After the turn of the century new stations appeared at Ocracoke Village and Fort Macon in 1904 and Bogue Inlet in 1905, bringing the state's final total to twenty-nine. By 1915, 250 lifesaving stations guarded the shores of the entire United States.

Along with improvements in equipment and rescue techniques, the architectural style of lifesaving stations underwent significant changes as the number of facilities increased. The structures of the 1880s were elaborated versions of the original cottage-style buildings of the previous decade, with such new features as enclosed watchtowers and larger rooms. Then in 1892 the Lifesaving Service adopted a standard plan for a shingled and towered station known as the Quonochontaug type. Examples of that style could be seen at the new Core Banks and Portsmouth stations, as well as at Oregon Inlet and Currituck Beach, where new buildings took the place of the old ones in 1898 and 1903 respectively. After 1900 the service also began building prototype facilities in the southern states, primarily North Carolina. One of those prototypes—a hip-roofed bungalow with deep eaves and a tall square tower—replaced the original building at Little Kinnakeet in 1904 and appeared at Fort Macon and Bogue Inlet. Another prototype originated at Chicamacomico in 1911, when a new station replaced the old one. The new model, which became known as the Chicamacomico type, repeated features from the Quonochontaug style—tall sloping roof, lookout tower, and shingles—but added columns on the front porch and double dormers on the roof. Buildings of that style soon supplanted the old structures at Poyners Hill, Caffeys Inlet, Kitty Hawk, and Nags Head. The Chicamacomico mode characterized the last generation of stations before the Lifesaving Service became part of the Coast Guard in 1915.

25. Portsmouth (1894)
26. Core Banks (1896; renamed Atlantic)
27. Ocracoke (1904)
28. Fort Macon (1904)
29. Bogue Inlet (1905)

NORTH CAROLINA STATIONS BUILT 1894-1905

Portsmouth Station. Photograph from State Archives.

Regardless of architectural style, all of North Carolina's stations enjoyed distinguished careers marked by many gallant and humane rescues. One such event involved the combined efforts of the men of Creeds Hill and Cape Hatteras stations in 1884 and earned for seven of them Gold Lifesaving Medals of Honor, the highest award made by the service and presented only for exceptional bravery. On December 18 the 491-ton barkentine *Ephraim Williams*, bound from Savannah, Georgia, to Providence, Rhode Island, with a cargo of lumber and a crew of nine, encountered a storm off Cape Fear, took on water, and floundered northward, perilously close to capsizing. Three days later the vessel appeared off Hatteras Inlet amid swells and gale-force winds. Lifesavers on the beach kept her under surveillance until she disappeared and then reappeared the next morning near Big Kinnakeet Station, where the men of Cape Hatteras Station rushed with their surfboat and equipment. Many of the Outer Bankers who gathered at the scene later declared the sea—crashing and churning over an outer reef and then across an inner reef to the beach—to have been the roughest that they had ever witnessed. Certainly no onlooker thought that anyone who, by a miracle, might be alive aboard the *Ephraim Williams* could be rescued. Waves tumbled over her decks, and only her masts remained visible from the shore. But suddenly a distress flag rose up a mast and fluttered above the vessel, indicating that survivors remained aboard.

Keeper Benjamin B. Dailey of Cape Hatteras Station ordered his surfmen to launch their boat. Standing in for one of the Cape Hatteras crew was Captain Patrick H. Etheridge, keeper of the Creeds Hill Station. One of Dailey's men had received word that his wife was dying, and Etheridge had agreed to take his place. Dailey manned the steering oar as the crew strained at their oars to propel the craft through the inner line of towering breakers that repeatedly raised and slammed the surfboat with jarring force. Miraculously past the first reef, the lifesavers rowed across the furious body of water, where their surfboat lunged ahead and

U.S.LIFE-SAVING STATION

United States Life Saving Station, Morehead City, N.C.

Pub. by S.A.Chalk

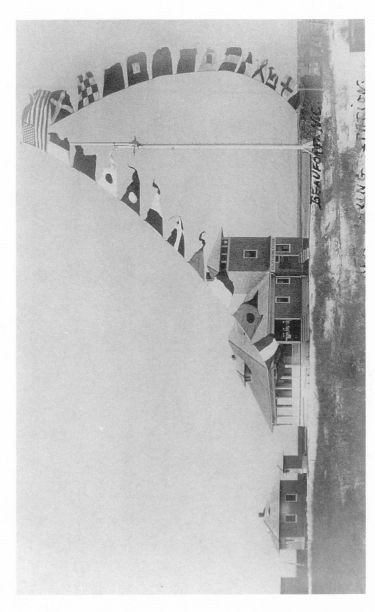

Two postcard views of Fort Macon Station at Beaufort Inlet, near Morehead City. Top from State Archives; bottom courtesy of Robert M. Topkins.

Second Chicamacomico Station (1911). Old building (1874), converted to boathouse, stands in rear. Photograph from State Archives.

crashed into the outer reef. There the breakers, seething and foaming, tossed the boat so high and vertical that spectators on shore could see its deck clearly. Landing on the other side of the waves, the boat leveled, and its occupants renewed rowing to the wreck. Arriving still hampered by high seas, they rescued the stranded sailors, who had begun building rafts. Had they used them the rafts probably would have brought the crew's deaths. Almost unbelievably, the lifesavers navigated back through the fury of the reefs and made a safe landing on the beach with everyone still alive.

The assistant inspector investigating the rescue reported: "I do not believe that a greater act of heroism is recorded than that of Dailey and his crew on this momentous occasion. These poor, plain men, dwellers upon the lonely sands of Hatteras, took their lives in their hands, and, at the most imminent risk, crossed the most tumultuous sea that any boat within the memory of living men had ever attempted on that bleak coast, and all for what? That others might live to see homes and friends. The names of Benjamin B. Dailey and his comrades in this magnificent feat should never be forgotten." For their heroic actions in saving the crew of the *Ephraim Williams*, the Lifesaving Service awarded the Gold Lifesaving Medal of Honor to Keepers Benjamin B. Dailey and Patrick H. Etheridge and Surfmen Isaac L. Jennett, Thomas Gray, John H. Midgett, Jabez B. Jennett, and Charles Fulcher.

Such feats as theirs continued along the North Carolina coast. In the same month in 1884 the lifesavers of Wash Woods rescued with their surfboat four sailors aboard the *Ario Pardee*, a sailing vessel loaded with cement that stranded and broke apart near the station.

In December a year later the schooner *Nellie Wadsworth* anchored in Hatteras Inlet to ride out a gale before passing into Pamlico Sound. The crew of nearby Durants Lifesaving Station kept her under surveillance. But about one o'clock on the morning of the sixth the beach patrolman discovered that the schooner had dragged her anchors and was aground about 120 yards from shore

Creeds Hill and, later, Cape Hatteras keeper Patrick H. Etheridge, recipient of the Lifesaving Service's gold medal for heroism. Photograph from State Archives.

and broadside to the beach. The Durants surfmen sprang from their bunks into the darkness and bitter cold and by three o'clock had set up their beach apparatus abreast of the grounded vessel, three miles from their station. They successfully fired off the shot line, tail block, and whip line. But after the sailors on the *Nellie Wadsworth* tied the block to the mast, the mast broke in two and the top half fell into the waves. Without the means to secure to the wreck the hawser on which the breeches buoy rode, the lifesavers improvised and tied a number of cork life jackets to the end of the whip line and sent them off to the ship. En route, however, the jackets became entangled in floating rigging. Sailor George Richardson jumped overboard and swam to the life jackets but succumbed to the cold water and unconsciousness before he could untangle them. Aware that the whip line had failed to reach its destination, the lifesavers tied their end of the line to the pony that had pulled the beach cart to the site. Driving the pony up the beach, they managed to haul the life jackets, the rigging, and the unconscious Richardson to shore. They disentangled the whip line and used it to save three more sailors, who clung to the rope as the surfmen quickly drew them ashore. A fifth man lost his grip on the line before reaching safety and had to be dragged bodily from the surf. The lifesavers revived all the victims. But Richardson, who suffered severely from exposure and intense cold, lost consciousness again and soon died. The men of Durants alternately carried and dragged the remaining four sailors, who were exhausted and unable to walk, to the station, where they received dry clothing and recovered with warmth, hot food, stimulants, and rest. Almost too weak to move, the survivors of the *Nellie Wadsworth* remained at the station for weeks before becoming strong enough to depart. The surfmen buried Richardson nearby.

The skill and reputation of North Carolina's lifesavers continued to grow and improve along with the postwar expansion of maritime travel and commerce. The Tar Heel surfmen participated in rescue operations or provided some assistance in virtually all of the sixty-five verified shipwrecks involving total loss of the vessels on the North Carolina coast between 1880 and 1889. Crews

from different stations frequently cooperated in lifesaving operations. In one case—the loss of the *Henry P. Simmons* in a tremendous storm in October 1889—lifesavers from four different stations
in North Carolina and Virginia took part in a joint effort to save
the eight men on board the schooner wrecked at the boundary of
the two states. Unfortunately, because of the distance of the wreck
from shore and the horrendous seas that thwarted the launching
of a surfboat, only one seaman survived. The same storm claimed
four other schooners: *Francis E. Waters*, at Nags Head; *Annie E.
Blackman*, at New Inlet; *Lizzie S. Haynes*, at Pea Island; and *Busiris*,
at Poyners Hill. In 1883 the men of Paul Gamiels Hill Station had
used the breeches buoy and the crew of Caffeys Inlet Station a
surfboat in separate efforts to save the sailors of the Italian barkentine *Angela*, wrecked en route from Cartagena, Spain, to Baltimore.
Skillfully employing their boat, which almost swamped, the lifesavers of Caffeys Inlet ultimately rescued the vessel's captain and
nine crewmen, but the ship sank. In May 1889 the crew of the
British steamship *Aberlady Bay*, which stranded at Cape Lookout,
made it safely to shore and received assistance from the keeper of
the lifesaving station. But subsequent efforts by tugboats dispatched by the British consul at Wilmington failed to refloat the
ship; it broke apart, a total loss.

   Shipwrecks in the 1890s exceeded the number of the
previous decade. According to the Lifesaving Service's annual
report of 1900, approximately 260 vessels stranded on Tar Heel
shores between the fiscal years July 1, 1891, and June 30, 1900. Of
that number David Stick has verified seventy-five as total losses.

   The wreck of the 1,231-ton steamer *Strathairly* off
Chicamacomico in March 1891 goes down in maritime history as
one of the worst tragedies ever to hit Hatteras Island. The English
ship en route from Santiago, Cuba, to Baltimore grounded before
dawn on the morning of the twenty-fourth and, battered by vicious
seas, began to disintegrate. A beach patrolman from the Chicamacomico Station spotted the vessel, fired a Coston light, and

returned to his post for help. But despite the best efforts of the lifesavers from three stations, fog, severe weather, and broken lines prevented success in the rescue attempts, which lasted almost all day. Eventually surfmen found ten bodies that washed ashore from the steamer. Nine others were never recovered, and only seven seamen survived the wreck. They suffered bad cuts and bruises from colliding with floating wreckage and other debris in the water. They took shelter at the Chicamacomico Station and, according to local tradition, left bloodstains that remained on the floors for decades.

Lifesavers had more success in saving the crew of the southbound three-masted schooner *Nathan Esterbrook, Jr.*, which, bearing a cargo of grain, stranded on an outer bar near Little Kinnakeet Station about a half hour after midnight on February 20, 1893. Within about twenty minutes Surfman L. B. Gray of Little Kinnakeet Station, riding a horse on his patrol, sighted the grounded schooner. His Coston light and two spares failed to ignite, and he galloped back to his station, sounding the alarm. At the station Keeper E. O. Hooper ordered Gray's horse hitched to a cart loaded with blankets, medical supplies, and equipment. He telephoned the Gull Shoal and Big Kinnakeet stations for assistance and burned a Coston light from the tower to let the stranded seamen know that assistance from shore was coming. He then boarded the horse-drawn cart and started for the wreck. His six surfmen (the seventh being at home) followed, pulling the beach apparatus cart. Before they had gone far, however, a crew from Big Kinnakeet overtook them with two horses, which they hitched to the cart.

The entire entourage of lifesavers had come abreast of the wreck by 3:00 A.M. and began setting up the beach equipment and firing the Lyle gun. The third shot landed the line in good position on the schooner. Captain George L. Kelsey and his eight seamen secured the block and signaled for the breeches buoy. But they attached the block too low on the mast and as the first man,

Second Mate Charles Clafford, was being pulled ashore the ship shifted and the hawser—already riding low—slackened even more. Consequently, the surfmen dragged Clafford through the rough water as they drew him ashore. He suffered severe internal injuries when he struck floating debris.

Convinced that the breeches buoy could not be used to save the other sailors, Hooper ordered the surfboat brought and launched. But high wind and surf, as well as a powerful current, prevented the boat from getting far. Thwarted again, the lifesavers still persisted and signaled the crew of the schooner to attach the block and lines to the lee bow for better clearance. Hooper also sent back to the station for the life car, which was then put on the hawser and pulled out to the *Nathan Esterbrook, Jr.* The car made four trips before the remaining seven seamen and Captain Kelsey all reached safety—some twelve hours after the lifesavers had begun their operations. No one from the three stations had stopped to rest during that period.

That night Second Mate Clafford died at the Little Kinnakeet Station and was buried the next day. His death, of course, was tragic, but the toll almost certainly would have been higher had the surfmen of Hatteras Island not demonstrated the tenacity, skill, courage, and sense of duty that by that time had become their hallmark. In fact, all along the Carolina coast the men of the United States Lifesaving Service were demonstrating how proper training, adequate equipment, and effective coopera-tion between stations had increased their effectiveness since the wrecks of the *Huron* and *Metropolis* in 1877-1878.

Such professionalism characterized Oak Island Station keeper Dunbar Davis during the storm that struck the southern coast of North Carolina in August 1893. The storm had been brewing in the Cape Verde Islands since the seventeenth. On the following day, as it headed west toward the Caribbean, it grew and became a hurricane that passed Cuba on the twenty-sixth. The hurricane came ashore directly at Charleston, South Carolina, killing hundreds of people and causing millions of dollars worth of damage. Ships in the vicinity had no prior warning, and a number of them were lost along with their entire crews. Winds from the northern portion of the storm also hit the Cape Fear region of North Carolina and sank or disabled five ships near the cape. The schooners *Kate E. Gifford* and *Enchantress* and the brig *Wustrow* went down west of Oak Island. The schooner *Three Sisters* floundered near Bald Head Island, and the schooner *Jennie Thomas* became disabled some distance south of Oak Island. Davis, who was manning his station alone because the active season did not begin until September 1 and the surfmen were absent, participated in rescue efforts for all five vessels. In what David Stick has aptly labeled the "long day of Dunbar Davis," the Oak Island keeper—employing volunteer surfmen and in cooperation with Keeper J. L. Watts of the Cape Fear Station on Bald Head—exhaustively went from wreck to wreck utilizing breeches buoy, surfboat, a team of oxen, and sheer fortitude to render assistance to the disaster victims. "By this time I was getting pretty fagged," Davis reported. "I had gone without food for two days and without water for 12 hours, and had been wet all the time." Not until the evening of August 30 did the tired, hungry, fifty-year-old keeper finally return to his station to collapse into the peaceful, well-earned sleep of a man whose devotion to duty was total.

Between August 1893 and August 1899 an average of one ship per week ran aground on the North Carolina coast. The Lifesaving Service filled its annual reports with many accounts of the heroism of North Carolina's surfmen during that period. Among the operations deserving special mention was that of the rescue of the crew from the *Charles C. Dame* at Frying Pan Shoals in October 1893. In that successful effort Keeper J. L. Watts and his crew from the Cape Fear Station rowed for eight hours in rough seas, in which they nearly capsized, to save the lives of Captain Samuel S. Grove and the seven sailors aboard the schooner trapped on the shoals. At Wash Woods Station in January of the following

year, Keeper Malachi Corbell and his surfmen had to build a firm
platform of logs and sand above the tide before they could use their
Lyle gun to aid the sailors of the stranded Norwegian bark *Clythia*,
heavily loaded with a cargo of marble. That operation took almost
all day, but the breeches buoy traveled to and from the wreck until
all seventeen seamen reached safety. In the following month the

Keeper and surfmen of Oak Island Station (*above and right*). Photographs from
State Archives.

schooner *Florence C. Magee* ran aground near Bodie Island Station. Keeper J. T. Etheridge with his own men and a crew from Nags Head Station abandoned the beach apparatus after an attempt with that device proved unsuccessful when lines became entangled aboard the ship. Undaunted, despite high winds and surf, they ingeniously saved the lives of the ten crewmen by tying a line to the stern of their surfboat. Lifesavers on the beach alternately held the line taut and released it to keep the boat on even keel between the huge waves, as the surfmen in the boat, unable to backwater with oars because of the powerful winds, rowed to the stricken vessel.

Dunbar Davis of Oak Island Station again proved his courage and leadership capability when he and his men saved the lives of eleven people aboard the Norwegian bark *Ogir*, which wrecked off Cape Fear on October 10, 1894. Commanding his surfboat, Davis had to contend with tremendous waves and great tangles of rigging and other wreckage to remove nine of the seamen to shore. He then returned to the bark to take off the remaining

two sailors, who earlier had been afraid to climb into the boat from the spanker boom. In December of that year Keeper F. G. Terrell of the recently built Portsmouth Station even attempted to effect a rescue using an old rowboat. Terrell spotted the schooner *Richard S. Spofford* stranded on the shoals of Ocracoke Inlet. But his station was not yet operational, having no equipment or staff. He nevertheless enlisted a number of volunteers, commandeered a rowboat, and rowed across the inlet to the village of Ocracoke. There he dispatched word of the disaster to the Ocracoke (Hatteras Inlet) Station on the other end of the island. Then he unsuccessfully attempted to persuade volunteers to row a yawl, in which five sailors already had reached shore, back to the schooner to rescue the three men still aboard. But the surfmen from Ocracoke Station arrived and with the breeches buoy rescued the captain and a sailor from the wreck. The third man had died of injuries.

In July 1895 (the inactive season) two hastily formed crews manning surfboats from two stations—Cape Hatteras and Creeds Hill—pulled alongside the wreck of the *J. W. Dresser* and together took off the nine crewmen. On the previous day the captain of the barkentine from Castine, Maine, en route to Cuba had misjudged the location of Bodie Island Lighthouse, and his ship had stranded on Diamond Shoals and broken apart during the night.

On April 26, 1898, the *George L. Fessenden*, a three-masted schooner bound from Philadelphia to Southport, North Carolina, with a load of stone, actually fell victim to two consecutive storms and lost two of her masts and most of her sails before she limped into New Inlet and anchored. Chicamacomico keeper L. B. Midgett observed the ship's disabled condition but saw no distress signals. He used signal flags to inquire if assistance was needed, but for some unexplainable reason the captain made no response to the flags. On the morning of the twenty-seventh, a northeaster began to blow hard, and the schooner snapped her anchor cables and drifted dangerously toward the beach. Midgett telephoned the New Inlet and Gull Shoal stations for assistance and led his crew to a site north of his outpost, where the *Fessenden* likely would strike the shoal. There, as soon as the vessel struck, lodged in the sand by the stone in her hold, the captain tumbled overboard and drowned. The remaining crew of six congregated on the forecastle as the strong current churning and pulsating along the shore drove powerful breakers across the schooner's decks. The sailors then crowded on the jibboom, and the surfmen fired their Lyle gun with good effect, landing the line directly on the boom. But the current kept the seamen from hauling it up, as their ship literally fell apart beneath their feet. Two died when struck by debris. Another drowned in the current. But the lifesavers dispersed along the shore and managed to save three sailors by pulling them from the surf using heaving lines. By the time the winds ceased their killing force, the *Fessenden* had disintegrated completely, leaving no sign that she had ever existed.

In the early morning hours of March 7, 1899, Keeper D. M. Pugh and the surfmen of the Gull Shoal Station battled ice and freezing temperatures to set up their beach apparatus and rescue the entire eight-man crew of the southbound schooner *Alfred Brabrook* before she broke up two miles north of their post. In August of that same year the hurricane known as San Ciriaco struck the Tar Heel coast with tremendous fury. One of the worst storms in the state's history, it destroyed hundreds of houses, wrecked countless boats and other property, and killed more than fifty persons.

Before the hurricane ended on the eighteenth, seven ships had been lost on the shoals of the Old North State: *Aaron Reppard, Florence Randall, Lydia Willis, Fred Walton, Robert W. Dasey, Minnie Bergen,* and *Priscilla*. Six others had vanished at sea, and the Diamond Shoals Lightship had been driven ashore. Along a lengthy stretch of the Outer Banks lifesavers frantically strove to rescue victims of the disasters. On the sixteenth—as the storm began venting its wrath on the Banks—surfmen from

Schooner wrecked near Cape Hatteras (1899). Photograph from North Carolina Collection.

Chicamacomico, Gull Shoal, and Little Kinnakeet stations managed to save three of the eight seamen from the *Aaron Reppard*. A line from the Lyle gun had reached the schooner, but the violent winds and seas had prevented the crew of the vessel from rigging the hawser for the breeches buoy. The lifesavers had to plunge into the surf to drag the three survivors ashore. The men of Big

Kinnakeet Station had more success when they used their breeches buoy to rescue all ten persons aboard the *Florence Randall*, which wrecked two miles south of the station.

The full force of San Ciriaco hit on the seventeenth, and powerful winds and high tide kept most of the lifesavers off the beach. On the following day Keeper Terrell and the surfmen of Portsmouth Station rowed their surfboat to the *Lydia Willis*, sunk at Ocracoke Inlet, but witnessed no sign of life remaining aboard her. They then proceeded to the *Fred Walton*, a moored hulk serving as a lay boat for steamers, which crashed and broke in two on a shoal. They took off the master and his wife. On their way back to their station they discovered that four seamen had survived aboard the *Lydia Willis* after all. Two of the six-man crew had drowned, but those remaining had found refuge in the rigging. After the storm subsided they climbed down and collapsed into an exhausted sleep, thus giving no distress signal when the Portsmouth lifesavers passed the wreck earlier. "They wanted to be carried to Ocracoke ware there friends was," Keeper Terrell later reported. "One was bad off. We used bottles of hot water and heated bricks to his limbs and soles of his feet. We stade with them all night and brought them out all right. Put them aboard Steamer *Ocracoke* Sunday morning which they took for thear homes, Washington, N.C."

The *Robert W. Dasey* stranded about three-quarters of a mile from the Little Kinnakeet Station. The surfmen hitched two mules to their beach cart, but it still required a long time to reach the grounded schooner because the cart and animals had difficulty moving through the mushy sand softened by the recent flooding. The lifesavers, however, did not need the beach apparatus, for the ship had wrecked perpendicular to and so high on the beach that the rescuers waded into the surf and helped the seven crewmen to safety by way of the jib stay hanging over the side of the vessel. The schooner could not be floated again, and she was permanently abandoned to suffer the ravages of wind, sun, and spray, eventually

Wreck of schooner *Robert W. Dasey* (1899). Photograph from North Carolina Collection.

to vanish. The Diamond Shoals Lightship fared better. She ultimately was refloated and returned to duty. On August 18 the men of Creeds Hill Station deployed their breeches buoy to rescue all nine of the personnel aboard the floating sentinel. Also on that day North Carolina lifesavers fired their Lyle gun, ran out their breeches buoy, and saved the lives of the seven sailors on the *Minnie Bergen*, a schooner bound for Cuba, which wrecked a mile or so from the Chicamacomico Station.

The most famous rescue associated with San Ciriaco was performed single-handedly by Surfman Rasmus S. Midgett of Gull Shoal Station. In fact, his actions rank among the most heroic in the annals of the Lifesaving Service. The barkentine *Priscilla* departed Baltimore for Rio de Janeiro on August 12 with a crew of ten sailors under the command of Captain Benjamin E. Springsteen and his son and mate William Springsteen. Also aboard were the captain's wife, Virginia, and their other son, twelve-year-old Elmer. The ship ran into San Ciriaco just before reaching Cape Hatteras. The *Priscilla* managed to ride out the vicious hurricane but became severely damaged, and she drove ashore about ten o'clock on the night of the seventeenth. As towering waves broke across her decks, the vessel began dissolving into pieces. A tremendous breaker tore Elmer Springsteen from his father's arms and washed him, his mother, brother William, and a cabin boy overboard. All four perished. Fifteen minutes later the hull broke into two parts, and the survivors crowded on the aft portion, which floated for about five hours before "it ceased to rise and fall." The persons trapped on the wreck knew that they had come to rest close to shore, but the seas remained so violent that they could only cling to the hulk and occasionally cry for help. Surfman Rasmus S. Midgett soon arrived on the scene. The Lifesaving Service's annual report gives the following graphic account of what transpired:

At 3 o'clock Surfman Rasmus S. Midgett, of the Gull Shoal Station, set out on horseback to make the regular south patrol, and when he reached a point about three-fourths of a mile from the station he discovered buckets, barrels, boxes, and other articles coming ashore, which satisfied him that there was a wreck somewhere in the neighborhood. The surf was sweeping clear across the narrow strip or bank of sand which separates the ocean from Pamlico Sound, at times reaching to the saddle girths of his horse, and the night was so intensely dark that he could scarcely tell where he was going, but nevertheless he knew that the patrol must be made at all hazards, and besides, the rapidly multiplying evidences of disaster urged him on. When he had traveled a little more than 2 miles farther he thought he detected the sound of voices, and, pausing to listen, caught the outcries of the shipwrecked men. He could see nothing of them or of the wreck, but dismounting and proceeding toward the edge of the bank he soon made out a part of a vessel, with the forms of several persons crouching upon it, about a hundred yards distant.

Here was a dilemma which called for the exercise of sound judgment and faultless courage. Midgett had consumed an hour and a half on his patrol before reaching the place, and to return to the station and bring back the life-saving crew was to sacrifice three hours more when every moment was precious. On the other hand, to undertake to save the lives of the shipwrecked men without aid was perhaps to throw away his own life and leave them utterly helpless until another patrol should be attempted, when all might have perished. Short time was spent in deliberation. He determined to do what he could alone and without delay.

Selecting the first opportunity when a receding wave permitted, he ran down as close to the wreck as he could and shouted instructions for the men to jump overboard, one at a time, as the surf ran back, and that he would take care of them. Then retreating from the inrushing breakers to the higher part of the bank, he watched his chance to approach the wreck again, calling for one man to jump. Obeying his instructions a sailor would leap overboard and Midgett, in each instance, would seize and drag him from the pursuing waves safe to the bank. In this manner, being compelled to venture closer and closer and more into danger, he rescued seven men.

During all these laborious exertions he incurred much danger from the likely chance that on each occasion he and his burden might be caught by the breakers and swept out to sea. But now came far greater demands upon his courage and physical powers. There still remained upon the vessel three men so bruised and exhausted that they were unable to do as the others had done. But Midgett was not dismayed. To save these he must go right down into the sea close to the wreck, take them off and carry them bodily to the beach. Down the steep bank into the very jaws of death three times he descended and each time dragged away a helpless man and bore him up out of the angry waters to a place of safety. Ten lives saved were the priceless trophies of his valor. Seven of the men were still able to walk, and these he sent forward toward the station, while the other three he took to a safe place, and after giving his own coat to Captain Springsteen, rode on to summon the aid of his comrades.

Keeper Pugh was on the beach when Midgett hove in sight, and upon hearing his amazing story ordered two of the surfmen to harness horses to their carts and proceed to bring up the disabled men. The other surfmen he directed to set up a stove in the sitting room and make a variety of thoughtful preparations for the welcome of the castaways. Imagination could hardly picture a more wretched company. When the vessel first encountered the breakers they were all sound men, well clad, with their clothing securely fastened about them; but the terrible buffeting they had sustained had stripped them almost naked, and their bodies were bruised, bleeding, and swollen, the sorriest case, perhaps, being that of Captain Springsteen, who had received a ragged wound in the breast, inflicted by the almost deadly thrust of a rough piece of wreckage. As the poor fellows hobbled or were kindly borne within the hospitable walls of the station the surfmen quickly took them in hand, stripped off their fragments of apparel, washed their bodies, gently dressed their wounds, and then clothed them in dry undergarments and placed them quietly in comfortable beds. It was the end of a splendid day's work, well worthy [of] the admiration of the whole people, whose brave and single-hearted servants of humanity had performed it.

For his heroic performance Surfman Midgett received the Gold Lifesaving Medal of Honor on October 18, the ninth North Carolina lifesaver to be awarded the medal. The first had been Keeper Malachi Corbell, who rescued two fishermen whose boat capsized on the outer bar near Caffeys Inlet on November 25, 1878. The other seven medals, of course, belonged to the men who performed the *Ephraim Williams* rescue in 1884.

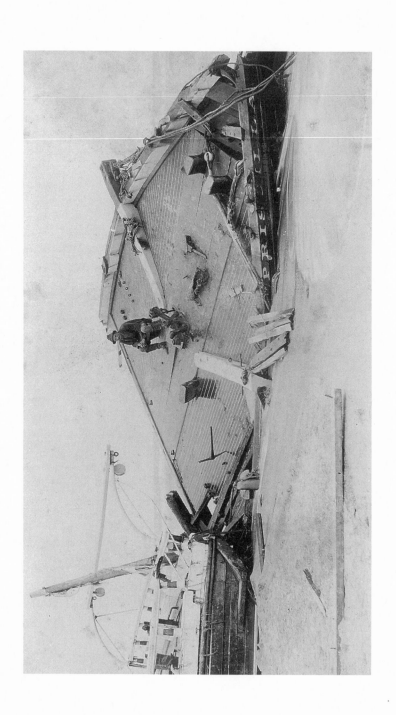

Wreck of the barkentine *Priscilla* (1899). Photographs from North Carolina Collection.

Wreckage from *Priscilla*. Photographs from North Carolina Collection.

Three more total losses followed the ship disasters caused by the hurricane San Ciriaco. One was the *Henrietta Hill,* a schooner that dragged her anchors during a squall and stranded three miles southeast of Portsmouth Station on August 24, 1899. The surfmen "were along side soon after she struck" and transported the crew, their clothes, and the captain's sextant, charts, compass, and clock to the station. "On the next day the surfmen helped to strip the vessel. On the 28th they ran out the anchors and tried to heave her afloat. On the 30th the revenue-cutter Boutwell tried to release her, the surfmen running the lines, but the effort was unsuccessful. On September 7 the surfmen helped to take the pump ashore, and the master gave up the hull as a total loss."

The schooner *Roger Moore* ran aground about one mile southeast of Big Kinnakeet Station on October 30. The station's lifesavers hastened to the site and were soon joined by the men from Little Kinnakeet. They did not deploy the beach apparatus because the schooner lodged so close to the shore that they were able to get a line on board without firing a shot. The seven sailors climbed down the line as the surfmen waded out to assist them ashore.

The nineteenth century ended with a horrible tragedy for North Carolina's lifesavers. The last wreck of 1899 was the *Ariosto,* which crashed ashore in bad weather approximately two miles south of Ocracoke (Hatteras Inlet) Station about 4:00 A.M. on the day before Christmas. The British steamship, laden with a cargo of wheat, lumber, and cottonseed meal, carried a crew of thirty, including the captain, R. R. Baines. The *Ariosto* was bound from Galveston, Texas, to Hamburg, Germany, via Norfolk to take on coal for fuel. That twenty-one of the thirty crewmen perished was particularly tragic because, according to a Lifesaving Service report, "there was in conditions not the slightest necessity that a single one should have been lost." Finding his ship surrounded completely by "white water" on the fateful morning, Captain Baines realized that she was about to run aground and attempted to back her away from the shoals. "The engines were working hard astern," the report later declared, "but were not able to stop the headway of the vessel, which took the bottom, and remained, as the master says, 'bumping and thumping in such a manner that it seemed probable her masts would come down.'" The seamen fired several distress flares, which were soon answered by the red Coston signal of a lifesaving patrolman. At this point Baines gave an order that proved fatal for twenty-one of his men. True, the captain had seen the Coston light, but he was convinced that his ship was wrecked not at Ocracoke but at Diamond Shoals, fifteen miles to the northeast. He believed that no surfboat could reach him in such turbulent seas and that he was out of range of a lifesaving gun. Besides, the "heavy seas on the starboard side broke away the three starboard boats, while the ship was constantly heeling over to the starboard, making the destruction of the boats on the port side likely to take place at any moment." Consequently, Baines ordered his men into the remaining two boats. Eleven manned the ship's pinnace and fifteen occupied the lifeboat, which accidently pulled away before Baines and three others could reach her.

That proved fortunate for them, for the lifeboat and pinnace both capsized in the breakers, and all twenty-six occupants began battling for their lives in the savage waters. One man, Seaman Elsing, a strong swimmer, swam ashore. Two others were hauled back aboard the steamer. The surfmen of Ocracoke (Hatteras Inlet) Station began setting up their beach apparatus and at about 5:45 A.M. fired the first shot. But it fell short, and the lifesavers hauled the line back. Along with it came a half-drowned boatswain, clinging to it, unconscious. The lifesavers revived him, and he told them that "the line fell across him as he was struggling in the surf; that he had sufficient consciousness to hitch it around his arm, and was thus drawn ashore." The rescuers saw other castaways struggling in the waves and waded out in water up to their necks to save them. They managed, however, to rescue only one, a fireman, who was unconscious but quickly resuscitated.

Seeing the men still on the ship as the sun rose, Keeper James Howard immediately set the international flag signal M K (*Remain by your ship!*) and resumed firing of lines with the Lyle gun. Yet, the projectiles continued to fall short until about eleven o'clock, when the ship had worked its way to within four hundred to five hundred yards of shore. The line finally landed successfully aboard the ship. Meanwhile Keeper Zora Burrus and the surfmen from Durants Station had arrived to assist the men of Ocracoke. By 2:30 in the afternoon Captain Baines and the five men aboard the *Ariosto* had been landed safely via the breeches buoy. But twenty-one of the men who had disembarked in the boats drowned. The Lifesaving Service's report concluded that "every man was saved whom the life-saving crews could by any possibility have rescued under the most unfortunate circumstances following the launching of the boats." The report ironically added that "if all had remained patiently on board, not one would have been lost." Realizing his mistake in ordering his crew to abandon ship, Captain Baines later testified in a document also signed by his surviving crewmen: "That such a lamentable loss of life occurred is not in any way to be attributed to the want of diligence, promptitude, or lookout of Captain Howard and staff, and we are unanimous in our conscientious declaration that their action in the matter was all that could be done, and is deserving of the highest commendation."

Chapter 5
Winds of Change

Despite the record of professionalism and commendable performance that North Carolina lifesavers had compiled since their
stations had been in operation, some citizens continued to view
the Lifesaving Service as a refuge for local political opportunists
seeking a government paycheck. Soon after the Civil War federal
funds became vital income for many coastal Carolinians. In addition to the salaries of the lifesavers and the expenditures that the
government made locally for the upkeep of their stations, United
States moneys went for staffing and maintaining lighthouses, post
offices, and weather stations. Federal weather facilities, established
in the 1870s, operated at Cape Hatteras, Kitty Hawk Lifesaving
Station, Portsmouth, Cape Lookout, Beaufort Inlet, and Wash
Woods.

Even after the enactment of civil service reform, which
began during the first administration of President Grover Cleveland, residents of the Tar Heel coast still looked to jobs with the
Lifesaving Service and other federal agencies as rewards for political loyalty. Previously Republicans had received the largest share
of the spoils. Former New York governor Cleveland won his initial

term as president in 1884, the first Democrat to hold that office since before the Civil War. Despite his stand for civil service reform, which even he had to amend for the sake of political expediency, his election led to requests for Lifesaving Service positions from coastal Democrats. Immediately following Cleveland's election, local politician W. G. Granberry of Currituck County wrote United States Senator Zebulon B. Vance (who opposed Cleveland's civil service reforms) for help in securing a position as district superintendent. "The battle has been fought and won," he informed the Tar Heel State's senator and former governor,

so say both parties by Gov. Cleaveland [sic], and after the victory then the division of the Spoils and right here Gov. do you or would you think it amiss if I should have my hungry eyes on some one of the thousand & one offices to be bestowed upon the millions of office seekers throughout this great county! Now one of the small offices that may & will be granted to some one in this district will no doubt be acted on in a greater or less degree by your approving service . . . and I want & most earnestly entreat you to do your best . . . to obtain for me the appointment of Superintendent of Life Saving Stations from Cape Henry to Hateras [sic] Inlet, most of the stations are in this State . . . & it is generally thought that the appointee should also be from this section. I think and know that you can do a power of good, if you will, and my old woman says you will, if you try, & of course I hope you will for I have been a strong Vance man.

Granberry's desire for an appointment went unfulfilled, and Joseph W. Etheridge—who had become Lifesaving Service district superintendent after John J. Guthrie died in the *Huron* incident of 1877—remained in office until his death in 1893. He was replaced as superintendent by Patrick H. Morgan of Shawboro, North Carolina.

In January 1886 T. M. Savage of Smithville (Southport) beseeched Vance to help him secure the position as keeper of the station projected for Oak Island. "Some time ago," he wrote,

I forward[ed] to the Hon. R. T. Bennett [congressman] my application for the appointment as Keeper of the Lifesaving Station soon to be established on Oak Island near this place. Mr. B. replied that he would give the matter due consideration in my behalf. He has letters from the prominent local members of the Democratic party vouching for me in every respect, particularly as being an old pilot in good standing, true of course and "at home" on the water. Notwithstanding the reply from Mr. B., I deemed it expedient to secure your valuable services in my behalf, believing that you take pleasure in assisting those members of the party who in the past have given every effort in the advancement of the cause of Democracy.

If you think it necessary I will secure a petition containing all the names of our citizens. Mr. Kimball, Supt. of the LS.S. may have the appointment, and he being a Republican, please permit me to suggest the propriety of [consulting] higher authorities in my behalf, for fear he might give it to someone in sympathy in politics. The present Keeper of [the] station at Bald Head, near hear [sic], has voluntarily given me his strong endorsement, and he being Republican shows whether or not I am worthy of your attention. If not impracticable would you be so kind as to [do] something about securing the appointing power's favor before you leave Washington.

Savage eventually received his appointment as keeper of the Oak Island Station. But the Lifesaving Service dismissed him from its ranks for procrastination and negligence in an attempt to rescue two sailors from the wreck of the schooner *Joseph H. Neff* about two miles southwest of the station in December 1890. One of the sailors died in the incident.

Such examples of incompetency, however, were not common. Overall, the record of the North Carolina lifesavers was exemplary—earning for the Tar Heel surfmen the gratitude and praise of many captains and crews who found themselves in dire need of their services. In a Beaufort newspaper on March 26, 1890, for example, Captain Thomas Hanson and Mate F. W. Robertson, on behalf of the crew of the *Joseph Rudd*, publicly thanked Keeper William H. Gaskill and the surfmen of Cape Lookout Station for their successful rescue by surfboat four days earlier. "We wish to express," they declared, "our sincere thanks and appreciation to Captain Gaskill and his brave crew of the life-saving station at Cape Lookout for the heroic bravery displayed by them in rescuing the crew of the illfated Schooner *Joseph Rudd*. The hardships and perils which they encountered in saving our lives will long be cherished and remembered." After hurricane San Ciriaco in 1899, the master and crew of the Diamond Shoals Lightship informed Superintendent Kimball on August 26 that "we wish to thank the Life-Saving Service for the timely assistance which was rendered us by the Creeds Hill life-saving crew. At 5 A.M. [August 18] we discovered the lifesavers coming to our rescue. The weather was thick and rainy and blowing a hurricane. All hands were in the rigging and the seas were breaking completely over the vessel. We were landed safely and taken to the station in an exhausted condition, where we were treated kindly by Captain H. W. Styron and his crew, for which we desire to tender our thanks." On August 29 Captain Boeman of the *Minnie Bergen* wrote Kimball: "I wish through you to return the thanks of my crew and myself to the brave keeper and crew of this station [Chicamacomico] for their prompt and valuable service in rescuing us with breeches buoy on the morning of August 18, during a severe gale of wind and rain. [Our] schooner was fast breaking up and seas were sweeping across her. We also thank them for their generous treatment while we stopped at the station."

The twentieth century brought a number of important administrative and technological innovations that made the Life-saving Service more proficient nationwide. On June 6, 1900, Congress approved the creation of an additional lifesaving district that included the coast of Rhode Island and Fishers Island. That area became the new District No. 3—the service's smallest. As a result, all the subsequent districts moved upward one number. Thus, North Carolina's district, which had been No. 6, became No. 7. During the first decade of the century the service also began

Oak staves salvaged from Hatteras shipwreck, 1900. Photograph from North Carolina Collection.

powering its surfboats and lifeboats with gasoline engines. The internal-combustion engine had been perfected to a degree that made it practical for employment in rescue craft. Its use greatly facilitated lifesaving operations, although pulling surfboats and lifeboats also remained in service for several years at some locations. By 1912 Congress had advanced salaries to seventy dollars per month for no. 1 surfmen and sixty-five dollars for the other surfmen. Keepers received one thousand dollars per annum, and district superintendents earned from nineteen hundred to twenty-two hundred dollars per year depending on the size of the district.

North Carolina lifesavers continued their distinguished record. One of the first rescues of the new century was the joint effort by the crews of Creeds Hill and Cape Hatteras stations to save the men of the British steamship *Virginia*, which wrecked off Cape Hatteras on May 2, 1900. The steel steamer, commanded by Captain Charles Samuels and bound from Cuba to Baltimore, carried a cargo of iron ore, a crew of twenty-four, and one stowaway. She ran aground in rough seas on the southeast point of the outer Diamond Shoals on the evening of May 2 about "9 nautical miles southeast by south from the Cape Hatteras Life-Saving Station and about the same distance east-southeast of the station at Creeds Hill." Captain Samuels attempted to free the hull from the shoals, but the *Virginia* remained fast and violently broke into three pieces. Samuels ordered all hands into the lifeboats. Two boats smashed into pieces when the crew attempted to launch them; but the port lifeboat, manned by fifteen persons and safely lowered away, made for the open sea. Seven sailors managed to get the port longboat over the side, but it quickly capsized, drowning six of them. The four men remaining on the bridge of the midship section of the wreck pulled the sole survivor back aboard using a bowline. The five, including the captain, then took refuge in the rigging, where they stayed throughout the night. On the following morning they managed to lower themselves back to the bridge. Fog and haze, however, obscured them from view of the shore. Desperate lest they go undetected, Samuels determined to swim from the midship section to the forecastle, where were stored oil and turpentine, which he intended to set afire as a distress signal. As the tide fell, "he jumped from the bridge and swam forward with all his power, beset by a strong current and with the sea continually breaking across the forewaist. However, he reached the goal, and encouraged by his success the chief mate followed." When night fell the two men ignited the oil and turpentine; but the wind and sea, as well as rain showers, periodically extinguished their fire. By dawn the thirty gallons of oil and turpentine had been exhausted—seemingly to no avail. Having passed two nights and one day without food or water, the victims were certain their end was near.

But the lifesavers of both Cape Hatteras and Creeds Hill had been alert and saw the signal. Keeper Patrick H. Etheridge at Cape Hatteras Station (formerly at Creeds Hill) sighted the wreck itself through his telescope at seven o'clock on the morning of the fourth, and he ordered his surfboat launched and telephoned keeper Homer W. Styron at Creeds Hill to do likewise. The boats cleared the beach at almost the same time and set sail for the outer Diamond Shoals. The wind blew a gale, and the sea ran high. Back on the broken ship, the wretched seamen had given up hope, but then about nine o'clock they spied in the distance the gleaming sails of the two surfboats. "For forty-two hours," one account read, "the poor fellows had endured hunger and thirst, and contemplated without sign of weakness almost certain death, but now that deliverance was at hand they gave way to tears—the brave man's last tribute to joy as well as to sorrow."

The boat from Creeds Hill arrived on the scene first, about a quarter of a mile from the wreck. Styron awaited the arrival of the lifesavers from Cape Hatteras and then conferred with Etheridge about the best method for performing the rescue. The keepers agreed that the Cape Hatteras crew would take the three sailors from the bridge and that the Creeds Hill men would save the captain and mate on the bow portion. Because the breakers were so heavy, the surfboats could not cross the shoals. They therefore proceeded under oars around the southwest point of the shoals, where both successfully accomplished their missions "without the most trivial mishap."

The surfmen then raised their sails for the trip back to the beach. They delivered the crew from the steamer safely ashore about five o'clock in the afternoon. The fifteen sailors who put to sea in the port lifeboat already had been picked up by the steamer *El Paso* bound for New Orleans, where the British consul provided them with care and assistance. Thus, twenty of the twenty-six men aboard the *Virginia* survived. But once again the Lifesaving Service's inspector testified that "had the entire ship's company remained on board none would have perished."

The first fifteen years of the twentieth century included many other rescues equally as noteworthy as that of the *Virginia*. The lifesavers of Cape Lookout Station, for example, distinguished themselves a number of times during that period. Led by Keeper William H. Gaskill, they saved the lives of five seamen from the wreck of the 660-ton barkentine *Olive Thurlow* in 1902 and two years later rescued with a surfboat the entire crew of the schooner *Joseph W. Brooks*. In February 1905 Gaskill and his surfmen—Kilby Guthrie, Walter M. Yeomans, Tyre Moore, John A. Guthrie, James W. Fulcher, John E. Kirkman, Calupt T. Jarvis, and Joseph L. Lewis (volunteer and former surfman)—all received Gold Lifesaving Medals of Honor for saving the lives of six seamen from the wrecked schooner *Sarah D. J. Rawson*. Suffering from the residual effects of influenza, Gaskill and his crew endured the dangers of smashing breakers, deadly floating wreckage, and a cold, soaking night afloat to save the lives of the sailors stranded on the 292-ton vessel that broke apart on Cape Lookout Shoals.

Keeper Eugene M. Peel and acting keeper Baxter B. Miller of Creeds Hill and Cape Hatteras stations respectively also earned gold medals—and nine surfmen silver medals—for their actions in the rescue of the twenty-eight crewmen from the German steamship *Brewster*, bound from Jamaica to New York with a cargo of fruit. On November 29, 1909, the vessel wrecked on Diamond Shoals, and the lifesavers from Creeds Hill, Big Kinnakeet, Cape Hatteras, and Hatteras Inlet stations came to the aid of the ship. A powered lifeboat (one of the first in North Carolina) from Hatteras Inlet took part in the operation, along with oar-powered surfboats from the other three stations.

Perhaps the largest number of persons that North Carolina lifesavers ever rescued at any one time was the 421 shipwrecked victims aboard the Portuguese barkentine *Vera Cruz VII*, which stranded at Ocracoke Inlet in May 8, 1903. Unproven suspicions later surfaced that the captain, Julio M. Fernandez, had been attempting to smuggle 399 refugees into the United States via the North Carolina sounds. But whether a smuggling plot was afoot did not concern F. G. Terrell and the surfmen of Portsmouth Station on the day the *Vera Cruz VII* wrecked. The lifesavers found themselves first occupied with quelling a fight that broke out aboard the ship and then had to transport the 22 crewmen and 399 passengers, including 23 women and 3 children, to safety during a strong northeaster with a high tide running. Keeper Terrell used both of the station's surfboats and hired more men with skiffs to help transport the victims ashore. He later reported that the "shoal was covered with water before we got them all off, had to be very watchfull to keep them from sinking the boats. Landed all about 9:15 P.M. by midnight had all under cover. All women and children slept in the station on beds and blankets and eat at the table. The people of Portsmouth was very kind and baked bread for us, we used 4½ bbls of flour and the 12 inst put 416 aboard cutter Boutwell to be taken to Newbern." In July the Portuguese chargé d'affaires dispatched a letter to the governor of North Carolina expressing his country's gratitude for the aid rendered to its subjects by the Portsmouth lifesavers.

The largest sailing vessel ever to wreck on the North Carolina coast was the six-masted schooner *George W. Wells*, out of Boston and bound for Florida, which wrecked at Ocracoke Inlet in September 1913. Struck by high winds, the ship lost all twenty-eight of her sails and foundered dangerously between Ocracoke (Village) and Hatteras Inlet stations. Surfmen from the latter, after seven unsuccessful attempts to secure a line to the vessel, finally used a line floated to shore by the crew of the schooner to set up their breeches buoy system and to save fifteen sailors, three women, and two children. Someone later mysteriously burned the hull of the *George W. Wells*, apparently as a result of an argument over her salvage, but authorities never charged anyone with the arson.

Most of the rescues discussed thus far involved vessels that became total losses. But for every ship that remained aground to disintegrate on the treacherous Carolina banks and shoals, there were numerous others that survived to sail again. The Tar Heel lifesavers provided invaluable service to their crews also. When the small schooner *George Taulane* ran aground on the day following

Schooner *George Taulane*. Photograph from State Archives.

the San Ciriaco hurricane, for example, the men of Core Banks Station boarded her, ran out her anchors, and successfully hauled the vessel afloat, allowing the crew, "with only slight injuries," to sail the schooner back to her home berth. In some cases the surfmen rescued sailors from vessels in peril, later returned them to their ships after bad weather had subsided, and then sent them on their way. When, for instance, the British steamer *Marstonmoor* stranded at New Inlet in 1900, the keeper at that station summoned help from Pea Island and Chicamacomico stations and succeeded in setting up the beach apparatus. But the master sent a note by the breeches buoy declining to land and requesting tugs to free the ship. The keeper called for the tugs but sent a message back to the captain to leave the vessel for safety pending their arrival. Five sailors then came ashore in the breeches buoy, were kept overnight, and returned by surfboat to their ship on the following day. A wrecking-company tug arrived on the scene and floated the steamer, which departed in calm seas.

In still another case, on December 19, 1910, two powered fishing boats bound from Southport to Harkers Island ran out of gasoline and floundered two miles southwest of the Bogue Inlet Station. Surfman J. W. Chadwick sighted their distress signals and informed Keeper Alexander R. Moore. "As night was approaching," Moore later reported, "I took a flag and went to the surf and warned them to the west of the bar while the men got the Beebe Surf boat. I burned a Costone Signal to let them know that we was coming." Arriving at the fishing boats—the *Romer*, captained by Eugene Yeomans, and the *Dixie*, by Clem Gaskill—Moore discovered that they had run out of gasoline and that the water near the bar at the inlet was too rough to allow them to approach. The two five-man crews anchored their boats and asked Moore to take them ashore. For better visibility, Moore waited until the moon rose then started for the beach with seventeen men in his surfboat. As he drew near the bar, he poured some oil borrowed from Gaskill overboard "to smooth the sea" and landed safely. The fishermen

Crew of Bogue Inlet Station man their surfboat. Photographs from State Archives.

spent the night at the station, and on the following day Moore retrieved their boats, found them some gasoline, and saw them off "through the Sound home."

The keepers' logs and the annual reports of the service are filled with hundreds such episodes involving lifesavers all along the Carolina coast. Some rescues or acts of assistance were little more than routine. Others included a large element of danger. Almost all involved some risk to the surfmen. Those activities, along with rigorous, regular training and frequent cleaning and maintenance of equipment and buildings, ensured that lifesaving stations remained very busy places for most months of the year. In addition to their official duties, the surfmen sometimes performed services—such as first aid, peace keeping, and a degree of public welfare and labor—for the residents of the communities near their stations.

The crew from the Kill Devil Hills Station even helped the two Ohio inventors Orville and Wilbur Wright launch their airplane on December 17, 1903—the first successful flight of a heavier-than-air machine. The lifesavers thus in effect became "the world's first aircraft ground crew." On the day of the first flight one of the Kill Devil Hills surfmen observed the brothers grasp each other by the hand just before Orville mounted the plane as pilot. "We couldn't help notice," the lifesaver recalled, "how they held on to each other's hand, sort o' like two folks parting who weren't sure they'd ever see one another again." Wilbur urged the station's crew "not to look too sad, but to . . . laugh and holler and clap . . . and try to cheer Orville up when he started." Using a camera provided by the Wrights, lifesaver John T. Daniels took the now-famous photograph of the first flight. When the Wright brothers returned to Kitty Hawk for further experiments in 1908, Wilbur, who preceded his brother, lodged for a time at the Kill Devils Hill Station and noted in his diary Surfman Bob Westcott's idea for building a perpetual-motion machine that would "practically eliminate the necessity of fuel or at least reduce the quantity to insignificant proportions."

As the Wright brothers' flight made abundantly clear, technology was on the move, and times were changing. Efficiency was becoming the order of the day, and the Lifesaving Service was caught up in the new movement transforming twentieth-century government and society. The continued existence of the service as part of the Treasury Department was in considerable jeopardy. In 1912 the federal government's Commission on Economy and Efficiency recommended that the Lifesaving Service be transferred to the Department of Commerce and Labor and combined with the Bureau of Lighthouses (formerly the Lighthouse Board), which had been moved to that department when it was created in 1903. The commission also recommended that the Revenue Cutter Service be abolished and its duties assumed by the navy. Republican president William H. Taft approved the commission's report and urged Congress to pass the legislation necessary to enact its provisions. But Congress failed to act on the measure before Taft left office.

Meanwhile, the Treasury Department, which opposed the commission's proposal, had drawn up its own plan for reorganizing the Lifesaving Service and Revenue Cutter Service. It proposed to combine both services into one military organization—thereby making both its lifesaving and maritime law enforcement activities more efficient and also heading off takeovers by the Department of Commerce and Labor and the navy. Its new combined force would have the benefits of military organization, accountability, discipline, and mandatory terms of service. The influence of political favoritism and patronage in staffing lifesaving stations also would be greatly diminished. Superintendent Kimball and Captain Commandant Ellsworth P. Bertholf of the Revenue Cutter Service prepared the reorganization plan. The chief problem, as they saw it, would be merging the civilian lifesavers, most of whom served only part of the year (ten months on the Atlantic and Gulf coasts), into a full-time military service.

In 1913 the Treasury Department sent its plan to the Senate, where it was introduced and then referred to the Commerce Committee. The full Senate did not consider the bill until just before its adoption in March 1914. The legislation then passed to the House of Representatives, where it languished until Democratic president Woodrow Wilson, at the request of Secretary of the Treasury William G. McAdoo, intervened and wrote the House requesting that the bill be included on its calendar as soon as possible. Some congressmen opposed giving military retirement benefits to United States lifesavers, but their objections found little support. On January 20, 1915, the House in a vote of 212 to 79 passed the bill establishing the United States Coast Guard. Eight days later President Wilson signed the legislation into law.

That statute made the Coast Guard a branch of the nation's armed forces, to operate under the Treasury Department in peacetime and as part of the navy during war or whenever the president might direct. For the first time, members of the Lifesaving Service (those who accepted enlistments) found themselves in a military organization. The benefits included retirement with three-quarters pay after thirty years' service, a concession already made to the men of the Revenue Cutter Service under an act of 1902. Vacancies for keepers and district superintendents would be filled by promotions within the service, thus ensuring experienced leadership, rewarding competency, and eliminating political patronage. Under the new system district superintendents became commissioned officers in the Coast Guard, keepers became warrant officers, the no. 1 surfmen petty officers, and the rest of the surfmen enlisted men. The reorganization law abolished the office of general superintendent of the Lifesaving Service but authorized the retirement of Kimball at three-quarters pay. He also continued to serve the new service as president of the Board on Lifesaving Appliances until his death in 1923. Captain Commandant

Bertholf became the commander of the new Coast Guard. The act establishing that service, however, did not change the ten-month duty period for surfmen, who still had to take leave without pay during the months of June and July. Not until World War I did they begin staffing lifesaving stations year-round. During the war the usual one-year enlistment for coast guardsmen was increased to the duration of the war, but not to exceed three years.

Although the establishment of the United States Coast Guard indicated that changes in lifesaving techniques were on the horizon, the routines of North Carolina's lifesavers did not alter radically or immediately. For the most part, the Tar Heel surfmen continued to operate as they had before the reorganization. Breeches buoy and surfboat were still the chief tools of their trade, and rescue procedures remained basically the same for about the next twenty-five years.

The *Sylvia C. Hall* was the first ship lost off the North Carolina coast after the Lifesaving Service became part of the Coast Guard. The three-masted, 384-ton schooner, en route north to New York with a cargo of lumber, wrecked near dawn on March 17, 1915, at Cape Lookout Shoals. Keeper F. G. Gillikin and his surfmen invoked the old and the new when they used a gasoline-powered and an oar-powered boat in tandem to bring the entire crew of the vessel to safety. Between the wreck of the *Sylvia C. Hall* and the United States's entry into World War I on April 6, 1917, the Carolina lifesavers, now coast guardsmen, repeatedly risked their lives in providing assistance and aid to ships and crews in distress. Most of their rescues involved sailing vessels, for the age of sail survived well into the twentieth century.

But World War I marked the beginning of the end for that era. Among the technological devices that worldwide conflict introduced was a sinister new naval weapon—the submarine. Inventors and navies had experimented with underwater vessels for years, but Germany became the first nation to utilize them effectively when it began dispatching its *unterseeboote* on missions

Lifesavers, ca. 1910, drill with surfboat and breeches buoy. Postcards courtesy of Sarah Manning Pope, Mount Olive, N.C.

to sink Allied shipping during the First World War. Throughout the war German submarines preyed on the ships of England and its allies as they crossed the Atlantic with American supplies and equipment for their armies in Europe. When the United States entered the conflict—after the Germans announced unrestricted submarine warfare on all ships in British waters and promptly sank the American *Housatonic*—the *unterseeboote* began attacking vessels and laying mines along the Atlantic coast.

The first submarine to invade North Carolina waters was the *U-151*, which left home in the spring of 1918 to lay mines, cut cables, and disrupt shipping. She mined the entrances of Chesapeake Bay and Delaware Bay, cut cables in New York harbor, and then headed south destroying maritime property and lives as she went. On the morning of June 5, near Knotts Island, North Carolina, the *U-151* torpedoed the British steamer *Harpathian*. The steamer's crew abandoned ship in lifeboats and were rescued by the British steamer *Potomac*. The U-boat (as submarines were called) continued to cruise the Carolina coast and sank three Norwegian steamships—*Vinland*, *Vindeggen*, and *Heinrich Lund*, all off Currituck Beach—as well as the *Pinar del Río*, out of Cuba with a load of sugar, near Nags Head. Passing ships picked up the survivors of those attacks, although the surfmen of Nags Head Coast Guard Station launched their surfboat and brought ashore the eighteen crewmen from the *Pinar del Río*, who had been rescued by a steamship en route to New York. The *U-151* left for home but was replaced by six other submarines, bringing to seven the total that operated on the East Coast during the war. One of these, the *U-140*, sank four other vessels in Carolina waters: *O. B. Jennings*, a tanker off Cape Hatteras; *Merak*, a steamer off Little Kinnakeet; *Stanley M. Seaman*, a four-masted schooner off Cape Hatteras; and *Diamond Shoals Lightship No. 71*. All the survivors reached shore in their own lifeboats or were picked up by passing ships.

But the one submarine that would remain forever indelible in the annals of the United States lifesavers of North Carolina

Captain Dröscher, commander of German submarine *U-117*. Photograph from State Archives.

was *U-117*. That U-boat had been laying mines and attacking vessels along the New England and Middle Atlantic coasts when she arrived off North Carolina on August 16, 1918. There her crew began watching for Allied ships and stringing mines across the shipping lane near Wimble Shoals, off Hatteras Island. On that same day the British tanker *Mirlo*, with a crew of fifty-two and a cargo of oil and gasoline taken on at New Orleans, rounded Cape Hatteras heading north to Norfolk. Captain Dröscher, commander of the submarine, spotted the tanker through his periscope and at 3:30 P.M. fired a torpedo that struck the *Mirlo* amidships.

William Roose Williams, captain of British tanker *Mirlo*. Photograph from State Archives.

The captain of the tanker was William Roose Williams, a veteran sailor. When the torpedo hit his ship, he attempted to beach her, but she began swinging to port, belching smoke from her side. A second explosion ignited more flames, and a third broke the tanker in two. Williams gave the order to abandon ship. Meanwhile, at the Chicamacomico Station tower lookout Leroy Midgett had sighted the initial explosion and called down to Keeper John Allen Midgett. "Captain Johnny" (as his crew and the local inhabitants called him) ordered out all hands, who hitched the station's horses to the wagon that carried the gasoline-powered self-bailing Surfboat No. 1046. The big draft animals pulled the

John Allen Midgett, keeper of Chicamacomico Station. Photograph from State Archives.

wagon six hundred yards to the sea, and the surfmen unloaded the boat. After three unsuccessful attempts, they finally got the craft into the high and dangerous surf and beyond the breakers.

While the coast guardsmen launched their boat, part of the crew of the tanker had managed to board two lifeboats and to get away from the burning wreck safely. But a third lifeboat capsized, throwing its occupants into the sea. One of the other boats attempted to rescue them, but suddenly another explosion erupted. Gasoline and oil floating on the surface ignited into flames, thus putting fire between the crews in the lifeboats and the unfortunate seamen in the water. Captain Williams believed the blaze too intense and the sailors in the other lifeboats too exhausted to save the capsized men desperately clinging to their overturned craft. Besides, the flames were so close, the captain later recalled, that "we were almost burning and it was only by the strenuous efforts on the oars that we managed to save our lives, the fire following us within a few feet for half an hour at least." The sailors trapped by the fire seemed doomed.

But then in the distance, toward the hellish scene came Captain Johnny and the surfmen of Chicamacomico. As Midgett's surfboat pulled abreast of Williams's lifeboat, the tanker captain told the coast guardsman of the sailors trapped by the fire and beseeched him to try somehow to save their lives. Midgett warned Williams "not to get too close to the beach as the surf was bad" but to wait for assistance in landing. Then Surfboat No. 1046 started for the *Mirlo* and soon disappeared behind a curtain of smoke.

As the lifesavers approached the stricken tanker, they saw barrels of gasoline explode aboard the ship, sending sheets of flame a hundred feet into the air. They felt the intense heat and choked on the rolling black smoke. Steering around the blazing oil slick, the rescuers found an opening in the inferno through which they sighted the surviving tanker crew, still grasping the gunwales of the overturned lifeboat. Nine of the seamen already had died, and the remaining six kept alive by thrusting their heads above the surface, taking a breath, and then resubmerging. As the coast guardsmen chugged toward them, the heat from the flames blistered the paint of the surfboat. "It was hot country," Leroy Midgett later remembered. Singed and scorched by the fire, the surfmen continued on, drew alongside the capsized boat, and pulled the six exhausted and hysterical sailors from the sea.

   Having saved those six, Captain Johnny and his men located the other two lifeboats and, with them in tow, started for Hatteras Island. Within two miles of the Chicamacomico Station Midgett decided to make a landing. He ordered the ship's boats anchored beyond the breakers. By making several trips the surfmen transferred the seamen to the surfboat and then landed them on the beach. The lifesavers from Gull Shoal Coast Guard Station and assembled residents of the area stood by to assist. The last survivor reached shore at nine o'clock in the evening, almost six hours from the time the tanker had been torpedoed. The vessel's crew spent the night at the station and then left for Norfolk the next day.

Zion S. Midgett, surfman at Chicamacomico Station. Photograph from State Archives.

Arthur V. Midgett, surfman at Chicamacomico Station. Photograph from
State Archives.

Although nine men lost their lives in the *Mirlo* disaster, the coast
guardsmen of Chicamacomico saved the lives of forty-two. They
had, Captain Williams later declared, "done one of the bravest
deeds I have ever seen."

On November 8, 1918, the British government awarded
gold lifesaving medals for "Gallantry and Humanity in Saving Life
at Sea" to John Allen Midgett, Zion S. Midgett, Arthur V. Midgett,
Prochorus L. O'Neal, Clarence E. Midgett, and Leroy Midgett for
their actions in saving the men from the *Mirlo*. The British Board
of Trade also presented John Allen Midgett with a silver cup in
gratitude. Three years later the federal government followed with
its award of Gold Lifesaving Medals of Honor. Then on July 30,

1930, in Manteo, Rear Admiral Frederick C. Billard, commandant of the Coast Guard, presented to the six lifesavers of Surfboat No. 1046 Grand Crosses of the American Cross of Honor. The Congress had approved the decoration in 1906 and stipulated that recipients be restricted to men who already had earned Gold Lifesaving Medals of Honor and that no more than twelve crosses could be issued in any one year. Only eleven were ever awarded.

As a conflict of global scope, World War I brought far-reaching and revolutionary political, economic, and social change. It also had a direct and significant impact on the United States Coast Guard. In its wartime association with the navy the Coast Guard improved its military performance and gained valuable experience afloat and in administrative proficiency, especially in its law enforcement arm. But in addition, the war sparked technological changes that ultimately altered lifesaving methods. In the decades following the conflict sailing vessels increasingly gave way to steam- and then diesel ships. With such innovations as radio communications, ship-to-shore telephone, improved navigational aids, and eventually radar and loran, the safety of maritime travel and commerce greatly improved. Advances in meteorology, or weather forecasting, made it possible for ships to escape bad weather. Larger, better constructed, and more powerful ships gradually began plotting their courses far out to sea, avoiding the treacherous coastline shoals that had frequently meant disaster for the sailing vessels of the nineteenth and early twentieth centuries. As modern shipping became more sophisticated and sailing vessels gradually vanished, the need for shore-based rescue facilities on every few miles of coastline declined.

World War I also demonstrated the capabilities of the airplane. Six Coast Guard pilots had served at naval stations, and in 1919 one of them, Lieutenant Elmer F. Stone, flew the navy's flying boat *NC-4* on the plane's first transatlantic (with stops) flight. In 1920 the Coast Guard opened its first aviation station at an abandoned naval air base at Morehead City, North Carolina.

Wreck of the G. A. *Kohler* (*above and right*). Photographs from State Archives.

The pilots flew six Curtis HS-2L single-engine flying boats lent by the navy. Headquarters designated the station's priorities as first lifesaving, then law enforcement, followed by assisting fishermen in sighting fish, and last surveying and mapping. The airplanes proved their value especially in locating ships in trouble. But as a result of the government's failure to appropriate funds, the Coast Guard closed the air station in 1922 and returned the airplanes to the navy. Yet a precedent had been set, and in the future the airplane—and ultimately the helicopter too—would play an invaluable role in Coast Guard operations. The range and speed of airborne surveillance and rescue, as well as those of modern cutters and motor lifeboats, eventually would conquer the obstacles of time and space that had thwarted the old Lifesaving Service.

Nevertheless, the rescue techniques practiced by the old service continued during the 1920s and 1930s. On December 3, 1927, the surfmen of Kill Devil Hills, Kitty Hawk, and Nags Head stations successfully used the breeches buoy to rescue twenty-four seamen from the Greek tank steamer *Kyzikes* (formerly called the *Paraguay*). On the same day crews from Cape Hatteras, Creeds Hill,

and Durants stations used both a gas-powered lifeboat and an oar-powered surfboat to save another twenty-four sailors wrecked aboard the Norwegian steamer *Cibao*. Two years later four Coast Guard crews commanded by Keeper Herman Smith of Bodie Island Station (formerly Tommys Hummock Station, north of Oregon Inlet) successfully employed the breeches buoy to pull to safety the twenty-one sailors and one woman aboard the Swedish steamer *Carl Gerhard*, which struck the sunken hull of the *Kyzikes* off Kill Devil Hills. In 1933 the crews of the Gull Shoal and Chicama-comico stations also rescued with the breeches buoy eight men and one woman on board the G. A. *Kohler*, one of the last large sailing vessels to traverse the North Carolina coast.

But such rescues were fast becoming events of the past. By the advent of World War II the old lifesaving stations and their then-primitive methods virtually had outlived their usefulness. During the war the Coast Guard (once again under the navy) confined most of its efforts to coastal surveillance and patrol. German submarines returned to hunt along North Carolina's coast and early in the war destroyed so much Allied shipping that the area earned the name Torpedo Junction. But by the spring of 1942 air and sea patrols by the navy and Coast Guard, protective maneuvers by convoys, and mines and nets that blocked submarine approaches and provided safe anchorage for ships all combined virtually to halt the destruction by U-boats. In May 1942 the Coast Guard cutter *Icarus* sank the German *unterseeboot U-352* at Cape Lookout with depth charges and sustained fire from its deck guns.

After the war the Coast Guard decommissioned or re-placed all its old lifesaving stations in North Carolina. The last of them (built before 1915) ceased operations in the 1950s. However, a number of the old buildings still stand. They have been converted into museums, beach cottages, restaurants, and, in one case, a real estate office. But the proud tradition of courage and humanitari-anism that those lonely outposts once symbolized lives on at the modern Coast Guard stations that presently operate on the coast.

Epilogue
The Tradition Continues

Ever the heroes on water or on land, by ones or twos appearing,
Ever the stock preserv'd and never lost, though rare, enough for
*   seed preserv'd*
                                                —Walt Whitman

On the site of the original Oak Island Lifesaving Station, built in
1886 at a cost of between four thousand and five thousand dollars,
sits a four-million-dollar state-of-the-art Coast Guard station,
which opened in March 1992. But on a knoll just across the road,
where it was moved to make room for newer facilities, the old
nineteenth-century station—now converted into a private beach
cottage—overlooks the operations of its modern counterpart.

The new Oak Island Coast Guard Station (the southernmost in North Carolina) stays fully alert for law enforcement and

---

The excerpt above is from Whitman's poem "Song for All Seas, All Ships,"
which appeared under another title in the *Daily Graphic* (New York), April 4,
1873, and in 1881 among the "Sea-Drift" group in *Leaves of Grass*.

search-and-rescue duties. Boats that serve both roles are berthed at its docks. A twenty-one-foot small boat, with a fast speed of twenty-eight knots and considerable mobility, performs primarily as a vehicle for local law enforcement but can also be used to tow small craft. A slightly slower but significantly larger forty-one-foot motorboat can navigate higher seas and greater distances to help ensure that the United States's maritime, immigration, fishing, and customs laws and regulations are enforced. The sixty-five-foot cutter *Blackberry* also ties up at the Oak Island Station, and she ranges far in carrying out the Coast Guard's dual mission. But the lifesaving workhorse of the station's fleet is the forty-four-foot motor lifeboat, which is designed, equipped, and used primarily for saving lives afloat. The vessel has self-righting capabilities and can operate in thirty-foot seas with twenty-foot breakers. Slow compared to its sister boats, it travels at a maximum speed of fourteen knots. But it has a vast towing capacity and can carry twenty-one passengers. With its durability it has proven a reliable and proper successor to the old surfboats and lifeboats that served the Lifesaving Service so well for many years. Recently the Oregon Inlet Coast Guard Station began testing a new forty-seven-foot motor lifeboat.

The new Oak Island Station's communications room contains the latest technical equipment for locating and conversing with vessels. The station's facilities include offices, a galley and mess area, duty quarters, and a conference room. Behind the new building stands the Oak Island Lighthouse (built in 1958), which is operated by the coast guardsmen and provides a powerful light as a navigational guide for ships. Nearby also is an electronics shop converted from a former communications center.

The thirty-three personnel manning the station enjoy comfortable double-occupancy quarters and a recreation room featuring a large-screen television, pool table, and table tennis. Because the Coast Guard expects its men to remain physically fit, the station has a well-equipped exercise and weight room with a whirlpool and sauna. The station encourages sports such as

The latest Oak Island Coast Guard Station opened in 1992. Oak Island Lighthouse (built 1958) stands in background.

Forty-four-foot motor lifeboat, the chief lifesaving vessel of the Coast Guard.

A present-day lifesaver: Seaman Scott Palmer of Oak Island Coast Guard Station.

volleyball and tennis and even keeps a "morale" boat for excursions and fishing.

Some distance north of Oak Island operates another type of modern Coast Guard station—the Elizabeth City Coast Guard

Air Station. That facility serves as a base for rescue helicopters and a C-130 cargo airplane. Helicopters can fly directly over rough seas to hoist victims to safety. The C-130 airplanes—also used by other military services to transport troops, equipment, and cargo—are not equipped to make rescues but perform long-distance searches. Their extra fuel tanks give Coast Guard crews ten to twelve hours of air time. The planes sometimes drop lifeboats or supplies to assist vessels in distress until a cutter or motor lifeboat can arrive on the scene. On many occasions Elizabeth City, Oak Island, and other Coast Guard stations in North Carolina have, individually and sometimes cooperatively, employed their technological capabilities and skill to perform a number of difficult and life-threatening rescues.

Although sophisticated stations have long since replaced the spartan outposts of the Lifesaving Service, the mission and mind-set of the men who save lives at sea have remained the same. Present-day coast guardsmen may utilize the latest in electronic surveillance and communications equipment and conduct search and rescue with the most up-to-date sea- and airborne craft. They may watch television in a plush, centrally heated and air-conditioned recreation room instead of playing checkers beside a wood-burning stove. But one factor has not changed: the late-twentieth-century coast guardsman, like his predecessor in the old Lifesaving Service, must still answer the call to risk his own life to ensure the safety of others.

Bibliography

BOOKS AND PAMPHLETS

Barrett, John G. *The Civil War in North Carolina*. Chapel Hill: University of North Carolina Press, 1963.

Bishir, Catherine. *North Carolina Architecture*. Chapel Hill: University of North Carolina Press for the Historic Preservation Foundation of North Carolina, 1990.

Bloomfield, Howard V. L. *The Compact History of the Coast Guard*. New York: Hawthorn Books, 1966.

Cain, Robert J., ed. *Records of the Executive Council, 1664-1734*. Vol. 7 of *The Colonial Records of North Carolina [Second Series]*. Raleigh: Division of Archives and History, Department of Cultural Resources, 1984.

Crouch, Tom D. *The Bishop's Boys: A Life of Wilbur and Orville Wright*. New York: W. W. Norton, 1989.

Hyde County Historical Society. *Hyde County History: A Hyde County Bicentennial Project*. N.p.: Hyde County Historical Society, 1976.

Johnson, Robert Erwin. *Guardians of the Sea: History of the United States Coast Guard, 1915 to the Present*. Annapolis: Naval Institute Press, 1987.

Lefler, Hugh Talmage, and Albert Ray Newsome. *North Carolina: The History of a Southern State*, 3d ed. Chapel Hill: University of North Carolina Press, 1973.

The National Cyclopedia of American Biography.

Parker, Mattie Erma Edwards, ed. *North Carolina Higher-Court Records, 1697-1701*. Vol. 3 of *The Colonial Records of North Carolina [Second Series]*. Raleigh: Division of Archives and History, Department of Cultural Resources, 1971.

Powell, William S. *The North Carolina Gazetteer*. Chapel Hill: University of North Carolina Press, 1968.

Saunders, William L., ed. *The Colonial Records of North Carolina*, 10 vols. Raleigh: State of North Carolina, 1886-1890.

Smith, Darrell Hevenor, and Fred Wilbur Powell. *The Coast Guard: Its History, Activities, and Organization.* Washington, D.C.: Brookings Institution, 1929.

Stick, David. *Dare County: A History.* Raleigh: Division of Archives and History, Department of Cultural Resources, 1970.

————. *Graveyard of the Atlantic: Shipwrecks of the North Carolina Coast.* Chapel Hill: University of North Carolina Press, 1952.

————. *North Carolina Lighthouses.* Raleigh: Division of Archives and History, Department of Cultural Resources, 1980.

————. *The Outer Banks of North Carolina, 1584-1958.* Chapel Hill: University of North Carolina Press, 1958.

Williamson, Sonny. *Unsung Heroes of the Surf: The Lifesaving Services of Carteret County.* Marshallberg: Grandma Publications, 1992.

ARTICLES

Abbott, Jacob. "Some Accounts of Francis's Life-Boats and Life-Cars." *Harper's New Monthly Magazine* 3 (June 1851): 161-171.

Bearss, Edwin C. "The *Mirlo* Rescue." *North Carolina Historical Review* 45 (October 1968): 384-398.

Couch, Danny, Noah Price, and Shawn Gray. "A History of the United States Life-Saving Service on Hatteras Island." *Sea Chest* 4 (October 1977): 1-62.

"The Loss of the Huron." *Harper's Weekly* 21 (December 15, 1877): 986-987.

Means, Dennis R. "A Heavy Sea Running: The Formation of the U.S. Life-Saving Service, 1846-1878." *Prologue* 19 (Winter 1987): 223-243.

Mitchell, H. H. "A Forgotten Institution: Private Banks in North Carolina." *North Carolina Historical Review* 35 (January 1958): 34-49.

FEDERAL RECORDS

U.S. Congress. House. *Economy and Efficiency in the Government Service.* Sixty-second Cong., 2d sess., 1912. H. Doc. 670.

————. *Estimate-Preservation of Life and Property from Vessels Shipwrecked.* Thirty-third Cong., 2d sess., 1855. H. Doc. 44.

————. *Letter from the Secretary of Treasury, Transmitting Report of Life-Saving Service in Reference to the Loss of the Steamer* Metropolis. Forty-fifth Cong., 2d sess., 1878. H. Doc. 58.

————. *Letter from the Secretary of the Treasury in Relation to the Act . . . to Provide for the Establishment of Life-Saving Stations on the Coasts of Maine, New Hampshire, Virginia, and North Carolina.* Forty-third Cong., 1st sess., 1874. H. Doc. 103.

U.S. Congress. Senate. *Letter from the Secretary of the Navy, Transmitting a Copy of the Record of the Court of Inquiry in Relation to the Wreck of the United States Steamer* Huron. Forty-fifth Cong., 2d sess., 1878. S. Doc. 26.

———. *Letter from the Secretary of the Treasury Communicating . . . Information in Relation to the Present Condition and State of Efficiency of the Life-Saving Service on the Coast of North Carolina.* Forty-fifth Cong., 2d sess., 1878. S. Doc 31.

U.S. Department of Transportation. Records of the Lifesaving Service, 1847-1915, in Records of the Coast Guard. Record Group 26. National Archives, Washington, D.C.

U.S. Department of the Treasury. *Annual Reports of the Operations of the United States Life-Saving Service.* Washington, D.C.: Government Printing Office, 1876-1915.

U.S. Veterans Administration. Records Relating to Pension and Bounty Land Claims, 1773-1942. Record Group 15. National Archives, Washington, D.C.

U.S. Works Progress Administration. North Carolina Writers' Project. Coast Guard Material, 1798-1940. State Archives, Division of Archives and History, Raleigh.

NEWSPAPERS

Boston Evening Transcript
Brunswick Beacon (Southport)
Commercial News (New Bern)
Economist (Elizabeth City)
Edenton Gazette
Edinburgh (Scotland) *Evening Courant*
Glasgow (Scotland) *Courier*
Glasgow (Scotland) *Journal*
Newbernian
News and Observer (Raleigh)
New York Times
North Carolinian (Elizabeth City)
People's Press and Wilmington Advertiser
South Carolina Gazette (Charleston)
State Chronicle (Raleigh)
Virginia Gazette (Williamsburg)
Virginian-Pilot (Norfolk)
World (New York)

PRIVATE PAPERS

Zebulon Baird Vance Papers. Southern Historical Collection. University of North Carolina Library, Chapel Hill.

UNPUBLISHED WORKS

Angley, Wilson, comp. "North Carolina Shipwreck References from Newspapers of the Late Eighteenth, Nineteenth, and Early Twentieth Centuries." Report, Research Branch, Division of Archives and History, Raleigh, 1991.

Friday, Joe D., Jr. "A History of the Wreck of the USS *Huron*." Master's thesis, East Carolina University, 1988.

Wright, David, and David Zoby. "Remembering Richard Etheridge and the Pea Island Lifesavers." Unpublished manuscript in the possession of the authors, Richmond, Va., 1994.

Index